# Authority of

## Unlocking Christ's Victory over Darkness

*Diane M. Neuman*

*1 Corinthians 2:11 - 13*

*[11]For what man knows the things of a man except the spirit of the man which is in him? Even so no one knows the things of God except the Spirit of God. [12]Now we have received, not the spirit of the world, but the Spirit who is from God, that we might know the things that have been freely given to us by God. [13]These things we also speak, not in words which man's wisdom teaches, but which the Holy Spirit teaches, comparing spiritual things with spiritual.*

# Authority of the Blood of Jesus

## Unlocking Christ's Victory over Darkness

Diane M. Neumann

*Authority of the Blood of Jesus* by Diane M. Neumann
Copyright © 2025 by Diane M. Neumann
All Rights Reserved.
ISBN: 978-1-59755-859-4

Published by: ADVANTAGE BOOKS™
Longwood, Florida, USA
www.advbookstore.com

All Rights Reserved. This book and parts thereof may not be reproduced in any form, stored in a retrieval system or transmitted in any form by any means (electronic, mechanical, photocopy, recording or otherwise) without prior written permission of the author, except as provided by the copyright laws of the United States of America

Unless otherwise indicated, scripture taken from the Holy Bible NEW KING JAMES VERSION®. Copyright© 1982 by Thomas Nelson, Inc. Kindle Edition. Used by permission. All rights reserved.

Scriptures marked NIV are taken from the NEW INTERNATIONAL VERSION (NIV): Scripture taken from THE HOLY BIBLE, NEW INTERNATIONAL VERSION ®. Copyright© 1973, 1978, 1984, 2011 by Biblica, Inc.TM. Used by permission of Zondervan

**Library of Congress Catalog Number: 2025951397**

| | |
|---|---|
| **Name:** | Neumann, Diane M., Author |
| **Title:** | *Authority of the Blood of Jesus* by Diane M. Neumann Advantage Books, 2025 |
| **Identifiers:** | Paperback: 9781597558594 eBook: 9781597558747 |
| **Subjects:** | RELIGION: Christian Life – Inspirational RELIGION: Christian Life – Spiritual Growth |

First Printing: December 2025
25 26 27 28 29 30 31 32   10 9 8 7 6 5 4 3 2 1

# Contents

**GOD'S MYSTERY OF SPIRIT AND BLOOD** ............................................................. 7
    *Intricately Created* ..................................................................................... 10
    *God Creates Unity Through the Blood* ............................................................. 13

**BLOOD OF THE LAMB OF GOD** ............................................................................ 17
    *The Need for Redemption* ............................................................................. 22
    EMBRACING ALL THE VICTORIES OF THE BLOOD ................................................... 26
    *Victories of Jesus Christ* .............................................................................. 28

**VICTORIES OF JESUS** ............................................................................................ 37

**FROM PHYSICAL DEATH TO RESURRECTION** ................................................... 45
    JESUS ENTERS PARADISE ....................................................................................46
    JESUS ENTERS HADES ........................................................................................50
    JESUS RETURNS TO HIS BROKEN PHYSICAL BODY ...............................................57
    COMPLETING THE CYCLE ....................................................................................60

**APPLYING THE BLOOD** ........................................................................................ 65
    SALVATION BLOOD ...............................................................................................67
    THE BLOOD OF REDEMPTION ..............................................................................70
    THE BLOOD OF RECONCILIATION .........................................................................75
    THE BLOOD OF RESURRECTION ...........................................................................85

*Diane M. Neuman*

# 1

# God's Mystery of Spirit and Blood

We who claim Jesus Christ as our Lord and Savior believe we are created in the image and likeness of our God (Genesis 1:26 - 27). Like God, we have three separate but united and interrelated bodies. Unlike God, one of our bodies is temporary. This temporary body is made of the same elements as our Cosmos. Like our Cosmos this body traps us in time and space for a season. As is true of everything within this Cosmos, this outer body disintegrates over time. The other two bodies are eternal. Our earthly physical bodies carry the other two while we live in this Cosmos. When we accept this truth of our created bodies, we begin to know, at a deeper level, this reality of our being. We learn this not by the evidence revealed and interpreted through our senses, but by faith. Eternal truth is not dependent on temporary reality evidence. Or another way of stating it is, what we know by our senses is understood through that which perishes and dies. As stated in 2 Corinthians 4: 18

> *While we do not look at the things which are seen, but at the things which are not seen. For the things which are seen are temporary, but the things which are not seen are eternal.*

While that which is learned and known in faith is understood as eternal living truth. Faith is the vehicle to move beyond the limitation of our physical body and enter the spiritual realm.

Our triune God is eternal. There is no end to him, nor is there a beginning. We were created in him and lived in him as spirit beings before we entered our mother's womb. Our eternal permanent being is both our soul body and our spirit body. Together they are eternal like our God. We know this for it is recorded in numerous places in the Bible.

Jeremiah 1: 4 - 6

*⁴Then the word of the LORD came to me, saying: ⁵"Before I formed you in the womb I knew you; Before you were born, I sanctified you; I ordained you a prophet to the nations."*

Psalm 139:16

*Your eyes saw my substance, being yet unformed. And in Your book, they all were written; The days fashioned for me, when as yet there were none of them.*

Ephesians 1: 4

*Just as He chose us **in Him** before the foundation of the world, that we should be holy and without blame before Him in love…*

Romans 8:29

*For whom He **foreknew**, He also predestined to be conformed to the image of His Son, that He might be the firstborn among many brethren.*

We were alive in our spirit bodies learning from God while living in God. God was instructing each of us to our individual destiny before being placed in our third body, our earthly physical body.

God created humanity in God's likeness and ordained us to become his family (John 1:12 – 13). He gave us free will to accept or reject membership in his family. God reminds humanity we have a choice of choosing eternal life or death (Deuteronomy 28). When we choose to seek God with all we are, we submit our wills to God. We surrender our authority and individual choices under the authority of God. When we follow this pathway, we are led into to a greater relationship with our eternal God. We learn eternal spiritual truths. Our spiritual bodies become alive at a greater level of knowing. When we choose to act and live outside of covenant with our God, we choose rebellion to the eternal order and harmony of the Cosmos. Since the actions, thoughts, and intents are outside of what supports spiritual life, these choices lead to chaos and death (Romans 5:12 -14). The avenue to eternal truth, faith, becomes corrupted when truth is sought outside of the covenant with God. Through surrendering our will to God, and obeying what faith teaches us, we grow in wisdom. As noted in Proverbs 9:10

> *The fear of the LORD is the beginning of wisdom, And the knowledge of the Holy One is understanding.*

Or again in Proverbs 8:13

> *The fear of the LORD is to hate evil; Pride and arrogance and the evil way and the perverse mouth I hate.*

Choosing to surrender our will and obediently following the ways of God is aligning with the pattern of righteousness and eternal truth embedded in our temporary world, our Cosmos. Choosing to function in one's own understanding not only bases truth on what is temporary, it is also to embrace what God hates. The beginning of eternal wisdom is embracing the "Fear of the LORD". It moves us beyond what is only revealed by physical understanding. As stated in 1 Corinthians 2:14

> *But the natural man does not receive the things of the Spirit of God, for they are foolishness to him; nor can he know them, because they are spiritually discerned.*

The soul, the second body of humanity, is the body that carries the record of actions, thoughts, emotions, and willful decisions of humanity. It is also eternal like the spirit body. Decisions and actions flow through the mind, heart and will centers of the soul body. When these actions and decisions are self-focused and self-serving, they feed pride. When this pride exalts a person and gives honor to themselves rather than God, it crosses over into rebellion. As noted earlier in Proverbs, this is considered evil by God. An atonement is necessary to return to a God honoring "Fear of the LORD". The blood was created by God to be the mediator to return humanity to a God honoring relationship with God and his creation.

We who have accepted Jesus Christ as our Savior have the unique opportunity to enter the Covenant of the Blood of Jesus. We can surrender our will to God's will and obey his directions. One direction is to be baptized in the Holy Spirit (Acts 1:5 & Matthew 3:11). Jesus stated to his disciples he would not leave them orphans when he returned to his Father God. Jesus would ask Father God to send the counselor. As stated in John 16:13 – 14

> *[13] However, when He, the Spirit of truth, has come, He will guide you into all truth. For He will not speak on His own authority, but whatever He hears He will speak; and He will tell you things to come. [14] He will glorify Me, for He will take of what is Mine and declare it to you. [15] All things the Father has are Mine. Therefore, I said He will take of Mine and declare it to you.*

We may have confidence in the Holy Spirit, our counselor and teacher. As we learn to move in greater faith and trust, we are taught within our spirit bodies through the Holy Spirit eternal truths (1 Corinthians 2:10 – 13). The unity Jesus Christ described in John to his disciples is the bedrock of this process.

## Intricately Created

God's wisdom is greater than what our minds can conceive (Isaiah 53:8 – 9 & Romans 11:33 – 34)). The balance maintained within temporary inert matter and living spirit to support life is still one of the great mysteries of life. Despite all the advances in medical science, humanity is still trying to determine the patterns and energy flow that keeps life in a being. When we examine this question from an eternal spiritual perspective, Holy Spirit leads us into greater wisdom.

When our creator God designed humanity, God placed a vehicle within the physical body that would connect it with our eternal spirit and soul bodies. This connecting agent is the blood. Something in the temporary body had to contain an element able to unite this temporary body with the eternal spiritual realm. This unity was necessary for the three bodies to function together. A spiritual avenue or channel allows the three bodies to communicate through what is permanent, the Spiritual Realm. For the Spiritual Realm is the source of life in the Cosmos. When instructing Moses about seeking forgiveness in the Holy Tabernacle, God told Moses this truth. As it is recorded in Leviticus 17:11

> *For the life of the flesh is in the blood, and I have given it to you upon the altar to make atonement for your souls. For it is the blood that makes atonement for the soul.'*

The "life" God is mentioning is the eternal life. God is declaring that corruption resting in the souls of people may be overcome by blood. Thus, blood carries a spiritual eternal component that covers and removes the part of the eternal soul that is not in alignment with the will of God. The spiritual property of the blood has the power and authority to destroy the seeds of rebellion growing in a person's soul.

How did this seed enter the soul and breed this corruption? God answers this question in Genesis 4:6 - 7. An eternal spiritual truth is given to Cain. Genesis 4:6 - 7

> *[6]So, the LORD said to Cain, "Why are you angry? And why has your countenance fallen? [7]"If you do well, will you not be accepted? And if you do not do well, sin lies at the door. And its desire is for you, but you should rule over it."*

Cain's emotions boiled in his soul body. God reminds him to stay under my will and obey God. If Cain chooses the path that honors God, God will accept him. God also warns that if Cain chooses to function outside of the will of God, an entity (sin) will enter his soul and live there. Notice, this entity has a desire and the ability to overrule the will of Cain. Humanity's will inhabits the soul body. In other words, accepting this entity aligns the person's will/choice to the entity's will. The person then becomes under the power of the entity rather than God's authority (Romans 6:16). When Jesus was discussing with the Pharisees their refusal to accept Jesus as being sent from God, he also declared the same nature of the entity sin. As recorded in John 8:34

> *Jesus answered them, "Most assuredly, I say to you, whoever commits sin is a slave of sin.*

Paul explains how this entity functions within the soul in the book of Romans. Paul describes the two natures fighting within the soul. One is the desire to obey God and submit in covenant with God. The other nature developed when his actions, thoughts, emotions, and attitudes were outside of the covenant with God. Like Cain, he opened a door in his soul to let this entity(sin) live in him. In Romans 7: 14 – 17 (NIV), the results are recorded.

> [14]*We know that the law is spiritual; but I am unspiritual, sold as a slave to sin.* [15]*I do not understand what I do. For what I want to do I do not do, but what I hate I do.* [16]*And if I do what I do not want to do, I agree that the law is good.* [17]*As it is, it is no longer I myself who do it, but it is sin living in me.*

Paul first judges his actions as outside of the spiritual law that keeps order and harmony in the Cosmos. Since Paul sees himself trapped in the actions he does not want to continue, he states he has become a slave to sin. Like God warned Cain, this entity called sin has overtaken Paul's will. Now Paul is subject to the desires and is weak to resist following through on fulfilling the desires of sin. In this struggle in his mind (another organ in his soul body), he argues with the desires. This arguing leads to self-condemnation. It does not break him out of the struggle.

God created a solution to the struggle before it even occurred. When the three bodies were designed, God planned for the blood to carry a spiritual nature that would overcome the entity (sin) trying to overpower the will of people within their soul bodies. Throughout Leviticus God instructed Moses how his people were to use the blood of animals to sanctify the altars and themselves for actions committed outside of the covenant with God. God honors our choices. He allows us to choose rebellion. Yet God is merciful, knowing that at some point people may choose repentance and seek to turn back to God and his ways. So, God created methods for returning to a living relationship with God. These ways are recorded in the Bible.

As mentioned earlier, corruption within the soul was the result of actions fostered in rebellion. When people begin satisfying desires outside of covenant with God, they may not realize they are becoming a slave to these desires. Because of pride and rationalization, the surrendering of the will to the entity is not, at first, realized. This is the illusion the devil used with Eve in the Garden of Eden (Genesis 3:11 – 13). Just as Eve noted, after the damage was done, she was deceived. People fall into the same traps and fail to recognize their will is compromised. As stated in the quotation in Leviticus, the blood provides the pathway for cleansing the soul body. In summary, the blood accomplishes two eternal spiritual acts:

➢ Blood is a vehicle to communicate and connect the temporal body to the two eternal spiritual bodies. This connection allows a person to function within the spiritual realm as well as the physical Cosmos.

➢ Blood offered to God is an agent to return a person to right relationship with God. It has the spiritual power and authority when applied in obedience under the direction of our triune God.

## God Creates Unity Through the Blood

The Bible explains how God created this eternal spiritual agent. Blood contains the spirit of God. God breathed his spirit into the inert clay body of the first being, Adam.

Genesis 2:5 – 7

> *⁵**Before** any plant of the field was on the earth and **before** any herb of the field had grown. For the LORD God had not caused it to rain on the earth, and there was **no man to till the ground**. ⁶But a **mist** went up from the earth and watered the whole face of the ground. ⁷And the LORD God **formed man of the dust** of the ground and **breathed into his nostrils the breath of life**; and man became a living being.*

The breath of life is spiritual and eternal. The inanimate dust of the ground now had an eternal connection to God. Thus, spiritual life could fill and occupy this temporary body within the Cosmos. The breath of Father God was released into the nostrils of Adam. Two things occurred. First, the life-giving spirit within the breath entered the lungs of Adam. The sacs in the lungs are filled with blood capillaries that pick up the spirit-filled breath and unite it to the red blood cells. The second thing is the heart pumps the spirit filled blood through the body, bringing life through the circulatory system. As Adam breathed out, he released God's breath back into the atmosphere. The spirit of God's breath remained in the blood of Adam. Later in the book of Job this is confirmed as recorded in Job 33:4

*The Spirit of God has made me, And the breath of the Almighty gives me life.*

Because it is God breathed, the spiritual nature of blood has a voice. For all creation was brought forth through the voice of God or spiritual sound vibrations (Genesis 1). Everything in our known Cosmos has a vibration or rhythm unique from the spiritual voice pattern of our triune God. Each has its own unique vibration and pattern based on what God breathed into it. As God declared a thing to be, God's breath was also in the declaration. We know it is true, that the blood has a voice, based on the word of God. As recorded in Genesis 4:10

*And He said, "What have you done? The voice of your brother's **blood cries out to Me** from the ground.*

The spiritual sound of Abel's blood, even after his death, was heard in Spiritual Realms. Though the physical body of Abel no longer supported life, the voice of his blood, which is spiritual and thus eternal spoke. This spiritual truth is again confirmed in Hebrews 12:24

*To Jesus the Mediator of the new covenant, and to the blood of sprinkling that **speaks better things than that of Abel.***

Where Abel's blood called for justice, Jesus' blood speaks louder and of greater spiritual truths. The spiritual properties of Jesus blood are different than the spiritual properties of Abel.

Abel is a son of Adam. Abel's conception brings the blood of Adam and Eve together. Both spiritual bloods are similar, from the same source (Genesis 2: 20 -22). Both were created in the same manner through the original spiritual breath of God. All the progeny of Adam and Eve bears the burden of consequences for their parents' rebellion in the Garden of Eden. One of the elements of the prophesy Father God gave as consequences of their rebellion includes a future battle. As recorded in Genesis 3:15

> *And I will put enmity between you and the woman, and between your seed and her Seed; He shall bruise your head, and you shall bruise His heel."*

Father God recognizes at some point the devil will produce through his seed and entity that will be against God and his plans for this Cosmos. Father God further limits the authority and power of the devil's seed to simply bruising the heel of his champion. This enemy's seed may injure and slow down his opponent but will not conquer him. The opponent is a seed of a woman; however, not of the bloodline of Adam. Thus, a promise of another form of impregnating the woman is declared.

When God ordained all was in readiness for this prophesy to be fulfilled, he completed this work. As recorded in Hebrews 1:1 - 2

> *[1]God, who at various times and ways spoke in time past to the fathers by the prophets [2]has in these last days spoken to us by His Son. His Son whom He has appointed heir of all things, through whom also He made the worlds…*

Jesus is the only begotten son of Father God. Luke describes the event. First Luke records the interaction with an Angel and Mary. As recorded in Luke 1:31 -33

> *[31]"And behold, you will conceive in your womb and bring forth a Son and shall call His name JESUS. [32]He will be great and will be called the Son of the Highest; and the Lord God will give Him the throne of His father David. [33]And He will reign over the house of Jacob forever, and of His kingdom there will be no end."*

The Angel is declaring the will of God for the child Mary will conceive. He is the one prophesied in Genesis, the seed of the woman. Naturally, Mary is perplexed at how this will happen. When she asks for clarification, the Angel declaration is recorded in Luke 1:35.

*And the angel answered and said to her, "The Holy Spirit will come upon you, and the power of the Highest will overshadow you. Therefore, also, that Holy One who is to be born will be called the Son of God.*

The mystery in this declaration is found in the role of the Holy Spirit. It is in Genesis when our untied God, the Elohim chose to bring spiritual life into a chaotic darkness, our Cosmos was birthed (Genesis1:1 -2). The Holy Spirit brooded over the darkness. Father God pronounced light. The Holy Spirit brought spiritual life into the light as he brooded over the chaos. Jesus Christ was present as the Word in this event as confirmed by John 1:4 – 5

*[4] In Him was life, and the life was the light of men. [5]And the light shines in the darkness, and the darkness did not comprehend it.*

Now in the moment of conception the Holy Spirit broods a second time combining his power of life-giving spiritual essence with the "light of men", the word of God. Jesus is placed in the womb of Mary as Father God speaks the spiritual truth of who he is into the physical body of Mary. This newly begotten being has the spiritual blood authority and power of original creative light. The second strand of Jesus' DNA is from Mary. She is of the blood of the progeny of Adam and Eve. Jesus Christ is truly the son of man and the son of God. Jesus' blood is spiritually greater and speaks in a different voice than the voice of Abel.

These spiritual truths are only the beginning of understanding of the spiritual truth of the blood of Jesus. The rest of this book reveals how this power and authority of the blood of Jesus is available to be used by God's sons and daughters. I encourage you to open your spiritual ears and eyes and explore the portion of this mystery God has chosen to release to his people.

# 2

# Blood of the Lamb of God

Father God reminds his people of the spiritual power of the blood when God ordained a new form of obedience. When God brought his people out of Egyptian bondage, he required an act of faith from each household. This was a new action for his people. God gave his promise of what this obedience would accomplish before it was to happen. As recorded in Exodus 12:12 - 13

> *$^{12}$'For I will pass through the land of Egypt on that night and will strike all the firstborn in the land of Egypt, both man and beast, and against all the gods of Egypt. I will execute judgment: I am the LORD. $^{13}$'Now the blood shall be a sign for you on the houses where you are. And when I see the blood. I will pass over you; and the plague shall not be on you to destroy you when I strike the land of Egypt.*

The power and authority of the blood of an animal, a lamb, would still the hand of the death angel. The people were to follow specific actions for this promise to be true for their household. Faith in God's words, and obedience were required of the people. Obedience to God's instructions was the faith action required to enact the promises. These steps, as recorded in Exodus 12:1 - 11 included:

- ➤ Bring a year-old male lamb without spot or blemish into your home for four days
- ➤ At twilight on the fourteenth day of the month slaughter the lamb.
- ➤ Place blood from the lamb, on the doorposts of the side and top of the outer door.

- ➢ On the same night roast the entire lamb: head, legs and inner parts
- ➢ Do not leave any of the lamb for morning but consume it all.
- ➢ What is left must be burnt
- ➢ Be dressed for travel when you eat it.

This pattern of believing in faith that God will accomplish what he promises united with obedient action is practiced each year. It is not only for remembrance of uniting faith with God's commandments and the blessing it releases. It is establishing a trust pattern in the lives of a nation through faith. The Passover is a forerunner of God's ultimate power to reconcile his creation to himself. The various actions during the Sedar meal are deep with symbolism of what has occurred and the promise of salvation to come. The power and the work of the blood is to be ingrained through this repeated annual event.

The power in the blood released in this ordained action of his people brought other blessings to the people besides freedom and protection from death. The power of God for protecting and providing for his people was evident through the sparing of the lives of the firstborn. Even the unbeliever recognized the power of their God. This awesome power was also frightening to those who had lost children and livestock. The Egyptians were glad to see the people of God leave so they willing gave them provisions. As noted in Exodus12: 35 – 36

> *³⁵Now the children of Israel had done according to the word of Moses, and they asked from the Egyptians articles of silver, articles of gold, and clothing. ³⁶And the LORD had given the **people favor** in the sight of the Egyptians, so that they granted them what they requested. Thus, they plundered the Egyptians.*

These physical provisions were not all that God provided through their obedience to this newly ordained act of worship. The people experienced healing. Not one person who left was feeble or ill. As recorded in Psalm 105:37

## 2: Blood of the Lamb of God

*He also brought them out with silver and gold, and there was none feeble among His tribes.*

The newly instituted action of worship, the Passover was to be an annual event to remind the people of the power of God that manifests in the blood in response to their obedience in faith. They were to remember and honor all the blood accomplished.

Later Moses brought forth the ten commandments. Instructions were also given to build the altar to God in the tent of meeting. Here the use of animal blood for sanctifying the altar and priests reminded the people of the great function of the blood to overcome the effects of sin. Another annual worship event was instituted to overcome the sin that entered the souls of God's people. This is known as the Day of Atonement. As it is recorded in Leviticus 23:26 - 28

*[26]And the LORD spoke to Moses, saying: [27]"Also the tenth day of this seventh month shall be the Day of Atonement. It shall be a holy convocation for you; you shall afflict your souls, and offer an offering made by fire to the LORD. [28]"And you shall do no work on that same day, for it is the Day of Atonement, to make atonement for you before the LORD your God.*

On this Holy Day the people of God were to embrace an attitude of repentance. They examined themselves and confessed sins that burdened their souls throughout the year. In identifying the sin, they were to break agreement with the sin. Each person was to ask God to help them overcome by the blood the willpower of the sin. Sacrifices as assigned by God were required by the priests. These were blood sacrifices of specific animals. As recorded in Leviticus 16:34

*This shall be an everlasting statute for you, to make atonement for the children of Israel, for all their sins, once a year." And he did as the LORD commanded Moses.*

Again, God is requiring an annual act of faith and obedience to remind his people of the necessity of recognizing and cleansing a person's soul of corruption. God was instilling a pattern into the corporate mind-set of his people. They were to be aware of the choices they made outside of obedience and faith in God which separated them from his covenant. God intended his people to recognize through the Passover, the power of the blood enacted in faith and obedience. They were to know the many blessings given through the blood sacrifice. In the day of atonement, his people were to know the separation from God they created by acts of disobedience. The solution to this separation was found in the sacrifice made in the temple by the high priest with the blood of designated animals. It was required yearly. These yearly feasts conducted in faith and obedience were the people's part of the covenant with God. This was to prepare a people for the completion of the prophecy in Gensis 3.

Hebrews explains the need for a better sacrifice. As stated in Hebrews 9:13 – 14

> *[13]For if the blood of bulls and goats and the ashes of a heifer, sprinkling the unclean, sanctifies for the purifying of the flesh, [14]how much more shall the blood of Christ. He who through the eternal Spirit offered Himself without spot to God, cleanse your conscience from dead works to serve the living God?*

As noted earlier, the blood of Jesus has greater power and authority than the blood of the progeny of Adam and Eve. The yearly requirement of atonement, repentance, and sacrifice of blood to cleanse a soul was accomplished with animal blood. This was a temporary cleansing; thus, it recognized as purifying the fleshly temporary body. The control of the will of the person's soul is broken when the people of God obeyed the entire process of confession of sin. The cleansing of the consciousness is a cleansing of the power and control the sin had in the mind and heart of the person. It is a deeper spiritual cleansing. Notice the purpose of freeing the consciousness is to return to serving the living God. The Blood Covenant with Jesus is a commitment to make Jesus Lord of one's life. It is a commitment to serve God rather than for personal gain. It is a change of heart and mind.

It is necessary to remember the spiritual limitations of our temporal physical bodies. What is created from the elements of the Cosmos is a container for the deeper eternal spiritual bodies. The blood within the physical body carries the power and authority of the breath of God so it can communicate and function with the eternal spiritual bodies. The spirit body and soul body are eternal. What is temporary has access to authority and power as it is embedded and transformed by the eternal spiritual power. God's breath gave that eternal property to the blood. As noted in 1 Corinthians 15:47 - 49 (NIV)

> *[47]The first man was of the dust of the earth; the second man is of heaven. [48]As was the earthly man, so are those who are of the earth; and as is the heavenly man, so also are those who are of heaven. [49]And just as we have borne the image of the earthly man, so shall we bear the image of the heavenly man.*

Adam was the first man created from the dust of the earth. Jesus Christ is the last Adam whose DNA contains the pure spiritual essence of Father God. As noted in John 1:4 - 5

> *[4]In Him was life, and the life was the light of men. [5]And the light shines in the darkness, and the darkness did not comprehend it.*

The original light declared from Father God lives in the blood of Jesus. This light overcomes all darkness and the products of darkness. The authority and power in this blood is greater than the blood in Adam's progeny or found in animals. It is eternal. The power and authority of Jesus' blood are eternal. Jesus Christ, the last Adam is also known as the heavenly man. He is the firstborn of the new creation (Colossians 1:15-18). His blood has the authority to cleanse the conscience, found in the soul body. It is not a temporary fix, needing yearly renewal as was true under the old Mosaic Covenant. It is a permanent removal and cleansing of the soul body. As noted in Hebrews 10:1 -4

> *[1]For the law, having a shadow of good things to come, and not the image of the things, cannot with these same sacrifices, which they offer continually year by year, make those who approach perfect. [2]For then would they not have ceased to be offered? For the worshippers, once purified, would have had no more consciousness of sins. [3]But in those sacrifices there is a reminder of sins every year. [4]For it is not possible that the blood of bulls and goats could take away sins*

## The Need for Redemption

The original rebellion of Adam and Eve opened a spiritual doorway in the soul body. As noted earlier, the entity sin now had access to corrupt what God created. This corruption is noted when God commanded Isaiah to declare and Jesus verified in John 12: 39 – 40

> *[39]Therefore they could not believe, because Isaiah said again: [40]"He has blinded their eyes and hardened their hearts, lest they should see with their eyes, lest they should understand with their hearts and turn, so that I should heal them.*

Humanity's will was compromised. The knowledge of evil entered the soul's mind. Adam and Eve determined they were naked (Genesis 3:7). At the eternal spiritual level, they recognized something was missing from their previous understanding. The knowledge of evil covered the intimate purity of God's goodness and hid it. Fear was born in their souls as they hid from the presence of God (Genesis 3:10). Later, in Biblical writings, we know what was missing was the Glory of God, also described as the anointing. Paul acknowledges this same spiritual understanding of covering as it is recorded in 2 Corinthians 5:2 – 5

> *[2]For in this we groan, earnestly desiring to be clothed with our habitation which is from heaven, [3]if indeed, having been clothed, we shall not be found naked. [4]For us who are in this tent groan, being burdened, not because we want to be unclothed, but further clothed, that mortality may be swallowed up by life.*

As Paul states, the temporary body was to be covered with a life-sustaining mantle. It is a spiritual mantle that covered and protected Adam and Eve from the power of evil. As Paul notes it covers the temporal body. This mantle or covering brings greater wisdom and connection between all three human bodies and the eternal Spiritual Realm.

When God is examining Adam and Eve, he asks whose voice were you listening to? As recorded in Gensis 3:11

## 2: Blood of the Lamb of God

*And He said, "Who told you that you were naked? Have you eaten from the tree of which I commanded you that you should not eat?"*

In other words, God is noticing his creation is listening to something outside of His will. God recognizes in them the seed of corruption as an alien vibration/sound to the harmony he created in his Cosmos. It comes from a source opposing the will of God for his creation. The voice of the fallen angel, Lucifer, known as the devil or Satan, is the source of rebellion in the Spiritual Realm (Isaiah 14:12 -17). By choosing to eat the spiritual fruit of the forbidden tree, they have opened access to the voice, power, and intent of chaos. This corruption now lives in the soul body. It is the spiritual fruit of the Tree of Knowledge of Good and Evil. As noted earlier, listening and agreeing with this alternative voice/sound leads to slavery to the entity. Adam chose this rebellion and now listens to an alternative spiritual voice. An eternal struggle within Adam's soul occurs as he attempts to return to the harmony with God, his Creator. As explain earlier, this eternal struggle will overtake all the progeny of Adam (Romans 7:10 – 23). This Tree of Knowledge of Good and Evil grows in the soul body of every person born into our Cosmos. Two voices may have access to the mind in the soul body of every human. Only that which is of greater spiritual power and authority can overcome this corruption.

To rectify this possession within the soul, a member of this new humanity must renounce and oppose the legal permission given to this entity to have a voice and position within the soul of humanity. In obedience, the will of this person is to be totally subjugated to the will of Father God. An eternal price will be required to break the power of the voice of corruption living is the soul. It will not be enough to simply break the voice and its power. To bring complete restoration to God's original plans, a redemption price is required by Heavenly Courts. Not only will the alternative voice need to be silenced in the soul of humanity, but a guaranteed method of accessing the voice of Godly directly is required. A spiritual replacement in the soul of humanity is required to seal the soul body. This sealing then reconciles the soul body with the spirit body and the physical body. The realignment of all three bodies to this sealing then returns a person to their original destiny. All three bodies are reconciled to their original relationship with God. In addition, a spiritual pathway or avenue for humanity to choose to only listen and obey the voice of God needs to be created. All these actions are to be in harmony with the Spiritual Realm. The righteousness and justice of the Spiritual Realm is to monitor these events within our Cosmos. Being in total alignment with the source of all life, the Spiritual Realm, is necessary to return humanity to its God created purpose. The Court of Heaven will record and approve the events as a permanent pathway for all humanity to choose. This solution is to remain under the legal guidelines of the Spiritual Realm. The patterns, cycles, and life-giving spiritual truths are to be upheld within this solution.

In summary, the Heavenly Courts will require a member of humanity to:

- Overcome the temptation of the voice of rebellion in the soul and defeat its voice
- Submit his will to God alone. All his decisions, actions, attitudes and emotions are subjugated to the will of Father God
- Be willing to be the blood offering to pay the price to cleanse the souls of those who also surrender all to Father God
- Overcome the powers of destruction by holding onto the life in the Spirit and Soul body until the price for all rebellion is paid in full in blood.
- Surrender his Spirit and Soul to Father God alone, allowing no other force to take them
- Reconcile the broken, corrupted humanity to the original intent and purpose of God. Rescue human destiny from the slavery of sin.

- ➢ Create a new pathway for others to follow to return to fellowship with God
- ➢ Become the mediator for all humanity as the firstborn of a new creation.

Before the foundation of our Cosmos, our triune God planned these events. Jesus Christ, who is the Word (John 1:1- 4) was set apart to complete these acts (1 Peter 1:20). When God determined all the preparation was completed for Jesus Christ to enter our Cosmos, this process was started (Galatians 4:4). A new covenant was born as these acts were completed. As noted in Hebrews 10:9 – 10

> *⁹then He said, "Behold, I have come to do **Your will, O God."** He takes away the first that He may establish the second. ¹⁰By that will we have been sanctified through the offering of the body of Jesus Christ **once for all**.*

This new covenant, the covenant of the Blood of Jesus was prophesied by Jeremiah and quoted again in Hebrews. As recorded by Jeremiah 31:31 – 34

> *Behold, the days are coming, says the LORD when I will make a new covenant with the house of Israel and with the house of Judah. Not according to the covenant that I made with their fathers in the day that I took them by the hand to lead them out of the land of Egypt. My covenant, which they broke, though I was a husband to them, says the LORD. But this is the covenant that I will make with the house of Israel after those days, says the LORD. I will put **My law in their minds** and **write it on their hearts**. And I will be their God, and they shall be My people. No more shall every man teach his neighbor, and every man his brother, saying, **'Know the LORD,' for they all shall know Me**, from the least to the greatest of them, says the LORD. For I will **forgive their iniquity**, and **their sin I will remember no more."***

This promise was achieved by Jesus Christ. Our soul bodies now have an opportunity to be renewed, cleansed and reconciled to our original destiny with God and his purpose in our time in this Cosmos. Now is the time to embrace all the victories Jesus Christ obtained through his actions.

## Embracing All the Victories of the Blood

Most of the modern Christian churches have limited their teachings of the power and authority of the blood of Jesus Christ. Most often, what is taught relates to the experience in the cross and the redemption gained through Jesus Christ as the Lamb of God. It is time to reexamine the full spiritual scope of the power and authority God placed in the blood when he created it in our Cosmos. As stated in the scripture, Isaiah 46:9 -10

> *Remember the former things of old, for I am God, and there is no other. I am God, and there is none like Me, declaring the end from beginning, and from ancient times things that aren't yet done, saying, 'My counsel shall stand, and I will do all My pleasure,'*

God's plans for the redemption of his creation, humanity, were developed before he placed our Cosmos in time. Being eternal, our triune God exists outside of the time he embedded into our Cosmos. God anticipated the plots and strategies of the enemy of God. Lucifer had already been thrown out of the Heavenly Realms (Isaiah 12:14 – 20) before humanity was created. God chose not to completely annihilate the rebel Lucifer. God simply planned to overcome the chaos and rebellion the fallen being would foment through the souls of those who chose to follow and traffic with Lucifer. He knows the end before he begins a creation. Throughout the Bible God tells humanity to use their wills to choose life or death, obedience to God's will or rebellion (Deuteronomy 28). God is specific about what blessings will be provided for those who choose life under God's authority and plans and those who choose rebellion and chaos.

The choice is real, and the results are declared clearly in Deuteronomy 30:15 -19

> *See, I have set before you today life and good, death and evil, in that I command you today to love the LORD your God, to walk in His ways. And to keep His commandments, His statutes, and His judgments, that you may live and multiply; and the LORD your God will bless you in the land which you go to possess.* ***But if your***

## 2: Blood of the Lamb of God

***heart turns away*** *so that you **do not hear**, and are drawn away, and worship and serve other gods, I announce to you today that you shall surely perish. You shall not prolong your days in the land which you cross over the Jordan to go in and possess.* ***I call heaven and earth as witnesses today against you, that I have set before you life and death, blessing and cursing; therefore, choose life, that both you and your descendants may live.***

God declared the creation, the Cosmos, to be witnesses in the Court of Heaven as he enacted this statute for humanity. God also declared a second witness as being the Heavenly Realm. Now the Courts of Heaven would be arbiters for all of humanity. God's declaration is the eternal law in both places. Our choices enact whether individually we live in prosperity and an abundant life or rebellion and perish. Notice rebellion is a process that leads to not hearing the voice of God. God warns of the possibility of being drawn away or tempted by the voice of the enemy of God. The result of obeying the voice of the enemy is hearts turning away from God and his plans for life under God's protection. The actions and consequences are clearly declared and recorded as statutes in Heavenly Courts. The results of the actions of Adam and Eve, the consequences of allowing the voice of the enemy access to the souls of humanity, are recognized in these statutes.

In summary, God gave humanity free will to choose how they would live in the Cosmos. Our individual choices would be recorded in the Spiritual Realms. Positive or negative consequences rested in the hands of individuals. In God's mercy, he planned a method for those who chose to return to righteous relationship with God. Our God is love (1 John 4:16). He seeks the best for his family. By his nature, he has provided mercy to withhold judgment and give opportunity for repentance. God has given us his written word, his prophetic word, and the Holy Spirit to guide us in all things as we choose. As recorded in Romans 8:28 (NIV)

*And we know that in all things God works for the good of those who love him, who have been called according to his purpose.*

We the believers in Jesus Christ as Lord and Savior have a responsibility to teach others all the truth of God's words. Let us bring forth the full truth to the unbeliever so the blessings and promises God has ordained for his people may be received.

# Victories of Jesus Christ

As noted previously, the completion of the prophecy in Genesis chapter three required multiple actions to destroy the power of the Tree of Knowledge of Good and Evil in the human soul body. A sealing of the soul was needed to shut the doorways into the soul by the enemy of God. For everyone who chooses to seek God, the Courts of Heaven required a righteous pattern for overcoming of the power of the Tree of Good and Evil. In addition, a balanced renewing of the spiritual connection of the spirit body, soul body and physical body to function as God originally intended was necessary. A new pathway for others to follow to enter the Spiritual Realm again was essential. In essence God was creating a new beginning for all those who sought a personal relationship with God. These multilayered requirements were met through Jesus Christ.

### Overcoming the Voice of the Enemy

Jesus battled the voice of the enemy all his life. He chose to live by faith, not by what was known through his physical body and human reasoning. He relied on the studying of scriptures to learn the requirements of God. He found the faith pattern of Abraham and his covenant with God. As Paul noted in Galatians 3:6 – 7

> *[6]Just as Abraham "believed God, and it was accounted to him for righteousness." [7]Therefore know that only those who are of faith are sons of Abraham.*

Jesus found himself in the promises of Abraham. As noted in Galatians 3:16

> *The promises were spoken to Abraham and to his seed. Scripture does not say "and to seeds," meaning many people, but "and to your seed," meaning one person, who is Christ.*

Jesus then began to live by faith, as Abraham did. He sought to turn his will over to Father God, in faith. It was in the submission to the will of God and acts of obedience Jesus functioned within the faith of Abraham. Through the prophetic writings such as Isaiah, David, and Daniel, Jesus found other patterns of faith. Jesus embraced these faith patterns and incorporated them into his life.

As a dedicated member of Jewish society, he functioned under the Mosaic Covenant. With his parents he traveled every year to Jerusalem to honor the high feasts. When he was twelve, he was found in temple questioning and being questioned by the spiritual teachers. As recorded in Luke 2:46 – 47

*[46]Now so it was that after three days they found Him in the temple, sitting in the midst of the teachers, both listening to them and asking them questions. [47]And all who heard Him were astonished at His understanding and answers.*

Even at a young age, Jesus sought the truth of the scriptures. By faith, Jesus sought God's truth through mediating on these spiritually inspired words. His understanding was not limited to the Covenant of the Law and the works it required. Because he embraced Abraham's pattern of faith, his trust was not in his own actions. This type of faith opened the door of revelation into the scriptures. When further questioned by his parents of why he was there, he responded (Luke 2:49)

*And He said to them, "Why did you seek Me? Did you not know that I must be about My Father's business?"*

Through seeking an intimate relationship with God as he applied scriptures, Jesus knew, God was his Father. We know this is true, since Mary and Joesph did not understand his meaning in these words (Luke 2:50). God honored the faithfulness of Jesus. Jesus was blessed with wisdom as he grew (Luke 2: 52).

Jesus was choosing to listen to the voice of God as revealed in the scriptures. Later, in his ministry Jesus declares, as recorded in John 5:19 – 20

*[19]Then Jesus answered and said to them, "Most assuredly, I say to you, the Son can do nothing of Himself, but what He sees the Father do. For whatever He does, the Son also does in a like manner. [20]For the Father loves the Son and shows Him all things that He Himself*

*does; and He will show Him greater works than these, that you may marvel.*

Again, as recorded in John 12:49 – 50

*⁴⁹For I have not spoken on My own authority; but the Father who sent Me gave Me a command, what I should say and what I should speak. ⁵⁰And I know that His command is everlasting life. Therefore, whatever I speak, just as the Father has told Me, so I speak."*

Jesus developed his relationship through faith with Father God to the level that the only voice he heard and responded to was the voice of God. The revelation wisdom Jesus received from Father God while he mediated on Scriptures was full of spiritual life. He shared the same handicap as all humanity of the Tree of Knowledge of Good and Evil living in his soul. What Jesus did was a complete surrender of his will to the will of Father God. The scriptures became alive with spiritual truth. He used these truths as his foundational rock to guide him. He did not judge anything by human wisdom, cultural norms, or societal accepted practices. By applying scriptures, seeking Father God above all else, he was able to ignore the voice of rebellion, Satan. This is the way of faith that Abraham patterned in his relationship with God. Jesus found the pattern in Scripture and applied it to his life.

We have evidence of this truth in the last two temptations Jesus faced in the desert after his baptism. Beginning with Jesus' answer to the second temptation, as recorded in Matthew 4:7 -11

*⁷Jesus said to him, "It is written again, 'You shall not tempt the LORD your God.'"*

*⁸Again, the devil took Him up on an exceedingly high mountain and showed Him all the kingdoms of the world and their glory. ⁹And he said to Him, "All these things I will give You if You will fall down and worship me."*

*¹⁰Then Jesus said to him, "Away with you, Satan! For it is written, 'You shall worship the LORD your God, and Him only you shall serve.'"* ¹¹*Then the devil left Him, and behold, angels came and ministered to Him.*

First Jesus answers the voice of rebellion with the truth of God's words. He stands on these truths in faith. He does not debate, defend, or expand the Word of God. The temptation to justify by Jesus' understanding is overcome. It is not his own wisdom, but the word of God, as he acknowledges it is everlasting life and spiritually true. In the second temptation, Jesus acknowledges the authority of God. He declares we are under the authority of God and will not use God's power to serves ourselves. Jesus will not take advantage of those at his disposal, the angels. Only under God's direction and will, does Jesus call on their aid. Jesus acknowledges and remains under the authority of Father God. Here is the bedrock of Jesus' faith. His trust is in the living word of God. This is why he can state, "I have not spoken with my own authority". This bedrock of trust in God's words grounds Jesus to overcome the temptation of acting out of his own understanding. Jesus has given his will wholly and completely to God. Jesus declares himself a servant of God's will.

In the last temptation, Jesus is declaring his position as a man created by God to serve and worship God alone. Jesus recognizes the Kingdoms of the Cosmos belong to God alone. God the creator and provider of life maintains and establishes these Kingdoms, not Satan. The authority is still in the hands of God. Jesus announces Satan is underneath him in the order of the Cosmos, not above him. By destroying the lie, that Satan rules the Cosmos, there is nothing left to offer Jesus to turn away from his mission. Satan leaves him. The voice cannot compromise Jesus' mission with temptations that have been successful with other people. Now the angels minister to Jesus. Jesus has totally aligned himself with God's will, purpose, and plans for the redemption for the Cosmos.

## God's Solution: A New Covenant

Jesus began his walk to the cross by initiating a new covenant with the representatives of humanity, his disciples. A covenant is a binding agreement where both parties offer something in an exchange. It is a legal spiritual agreement recorded in the Courts of Heaven. Luke records this intent in his gospel as revealed in Luke 22:15 - 16

> *$^{15}$Then He said to them, "With fervent desire I have desired to eat this Passover with you before I suffer. $^{16}$For I say to you, I will no longer eat of it until it is fulfilled in the kingdom of God."*

This fulfillment was the total completion of all that was required to reconcile humanity to its original destiny. The spiritual truths of his actions were to be recognized, accepted, and recorded in the eternal Kingdom of God. The Passover using the blood of animals was to be overcome and replaced with the blood of Jesus, the Lamb of God. For this to meet all legal requirements within the Heavenly Court, the old covenant was to pass away for the new covenant to be established. The new covenant was to be declared in the Cosmos. This transfer of benefits from Mosaic Covenant was to be in harmony with all the statutes of Heavenly Courts. All previous prophesies were to be met in the actions of Jesus.

Jesus interrupted the ritual of the Passover with new actions and words to accomplish this creation of the new covenant. Remember God declared that Heavenly Realms and the Cosmos were to be the witnesses in the Court of Heaven for choices and actions of individuals. As a human, what Jesus does to fulfill the requirement by the Heavenly Courts, to restore humanity to its original purpose is witnessed in both places. Jesus' heart intent, his surrendered will, and his obedience to God's plans are witnessed to be brought to the Courts of Heaven.

At what we now call the Last Supper the principles of the Covenant of the Blood of Jesus are established. The actions of the disciples and Jesus are a spiritual exchange. As recorded in Matthew 26:26 – 30

> *$^{26}$And as they were eating, Jesus took bread, blessed and broke it, and gave it to the disciples and said, "Take, eat; this is My body." $^{27}$Then He took the cup, and gave thanks, and gave it to them, saying, "Drink from it, all of you. $^{28}$"For this is My blood of the new covenant, which is shed for many for the remission of sins.*

By offering His body in the form of bread, Jesus was telling them he was becoming one with their physical bodies. Spiritually, the exchange was, what I do with my physical body will be also true for your physical body. The disciples are representatives of humanity offering their bondage to the Tree of Knowledge of Good and Evil, manifested in their physical and soul bodies. The action of taking and eating the bread is an agreement to the conditions of the covenant. Bondage in the soul is exchanged for the benefits of Jesus' sacrifice of his human body. Earlier in his work, Jesus declared a spiritual truth of the bread and body. As recorded in John 6:53 – 54

> *$^{53}$Then Jesus said to them, "Most assuredly, I say to you, unless you eat the flesh of the Son of Man and drink His blood, you have no life in you. $^{54}$"Whoever eats My flesh and drinks My blood has eternal life, and I will raise him up at the last day. $^{55}$For My flesh is food indeed, and My blood is drink indeed. $^{56}$He who eats My flesh and drinks My blood abides in Me, and I in him.*

Now Jesus is enacting this truth to overcome the old covenant of the blood of animals with his body and blood. Under the new covenant we, the faith believers will abide in Jesus, and he will abide in us. As the bread was consumed and joined with the disciples' bodies, so would the risen Jesus enter their soul bodies. What was in the cup that they all drank was representative for Jesus' blood. Again, he was initiating a unity between the disciples and what Jesus was going to offer to God. This cup represented Jesus Blood. It also contained spiritually humanity's offering in the exchange of covenant. Humanity, by way of the disciples, were offering their own sin-corrupted blood in their soul bodies. We know this is true for Jesus stated he was offering his blood for the remission of sins (Matthew 26:28). The covenant agreement was to be agreed upon before the actions of Jesus. All was set so it could be recorded and witnessed in the Courts of Heaven.

## Victory Over the Voice of the Enemy

The purpose and process of the covenantal exchanges is recorded in 2 Corinthians 5:21

> *For He made Him who knew no sin to be sin for us, that we might become the righteousness of God in Him.*

Our Triune God, in agreement with himself, created a plan to redeem all of humanity. Jesus willingly gave himself to the plan. The first part was to walk in total faith and obedience to the authority and power of Father God while living in a human body. He accomplished this. He was sinless by obedience and faith. The next part was for Jesus to be filled with the corruption of sin in his soul. He was to become our sin so we could exchange our sin for his righteousness. It is a covenant agreement.

In Gethsemane, when Jesus is in the first stage of redeeming humanity's position in the Cosmos, Satan attacks again. The exchange with his disciples to take and imbibe their sin-corruption spiritually, was already affecting Jesus' soul body. As recorded in Matthew 26:37 – 38

> *[37]And He took with Him Peter and the two sons of Zebedee, and He began to be sorrowful and deeply distressed. [38]Then He said to them, "My soul is exceedingly sorrowful, even to death. Stay here and watch with Me."*

Jesus was committed to complete the work necessary to redeem humanity. Many times, he told his disciples he would be turned over to the religious and governmental authorities to be put to death (Matthew 16:21 & Luke 9:44). He even told them he would be crucified (Matthew 20:18 – 19). Jesus taught them he would also rise after three days of death (Mark 10:33). Recently they witnessed Jesus' victory over death in the raising of Lazarus. He was dead four days. Yet they did not understand and were afraid to ask what he meant about his own death (Mark 9: 30 – 32). In faith and submission to the will of God, Jesus was committed to the total completion of the prophesy of Isaiah 53. As recorded in Hebrews 12:2

> *Looking unto Jesus, the author and finisher of our faith, who for the joy set before Him endured the cross, despising the shame, and has sat down at the right hand of God.*

Jesus was determined. His mind and will were focused on the completion of this work. He found joy in doing the will of God, even in this type of death. This sorrow was not his but a result of the covenant exchange with the disciples. The distress was a result of Satan seeing the sin now in Jesus' soul and attempting to overpower Jesus' will with this sin. Satan was attempting to use the sorrow in his soul to bring death back as a reality to fear into Jesus' consciousness. Satan believed this fear would give him power to take Jesus' life when Satan chose to bring that death.

Jesus' answer was to pray under the authority of the word of God. As noted in Hebrews 4:12, when in spiritual battle the word of God has the power to cut through what is attempting to bind the soul.

> *[12]For the word of God is living and powerful. Sharper than any two-edged sword, piercing even to the division of soul and spirit, and of joints and marrow, and is a discerner of the thoughts and intents of the heart.*

Jesus applied this living power in prayer. He used it to cut the connection between his will and the entity in his soul trying to master Jesus' will. Jesus called to Father God and the unity he had with him, to fill his spirit body to overcome this pull of death. He asked his disciples to support his battle in prayer. He knew Satan was trying to break his will from obeying God. We know this by what is recorded next in Matthew 26:39

> *He went a little farther and fell on His face, and prayed, saying, "O My Father, if it is possible, let this cup pass from Me; nevertheless, not as I will, but as You will."*

The cup was the realization of the weight of sin on his soul and the power to pull his will from the will of God. Remember, he was not personally familiar with the presence of sin in his soul. In this battle, Jesus fights to stay focused on the will of God as he applies the living word of God to conquer his soul. Just like the last temptation, Jesus is placing the power of Satan underneath the authority of the will of God.

Luke describes this struggle further. After speaking to the disciples again, Jesus returned to the Garden to pray a second time. He is still struggling to master what is in his soul and put it under the authority of Father God's Word and will. His first prayer is answered as an angel is sent to strengthen him. Luke describes it in Luke 22:43 – 44

> *⁴³Then an angel appeared to Him from heaven, strengthening Him. ⁴⁴And being in agony, He prayed more earnestly. Then His sweat became like great drops of blood falling down to the ground.*

As Jesus fights within his consciousness to overcome the temptation of sin to master Jesus' will, He begins to sweat blood. This first blood is a sign Jesus has won the battle over the voice of the enemy in his consciousness. Further evidence of his victory is Jesus walked with conviction out of the Garden. Since this is being witnessed in the Cosmos and the Spiritual Realm, the event is recorded in the Courts of Heaven as a victory for Jesus, sealed in his blood. The blood now contains the authority and power to overcome the voice of the enemy attempting to speak in the souls of people.

# 3

# Victories of Jesus

At Gethsemane, Jesus was arrested and taken to trial. As mentioned earlier, Jesus was committed to redeeming humanity to its original purpose and relationship with God. He was not a victim. He was not a meek lamb simply submitting to the verdicts of man's courts. As he stated earlier, no man could take his life. As recorded in John10:17 – 18

> *[17]Therefore, My Father loves Me, because I lay down My life that I may take it again. [18]No one takes it from Me, but I lay it down of Myself. I have the power to lay it down, and I have power to take it again. This command I have received from My Father.*

Jesus had just won the victory over the voice of the enemy. He knew spiritual truth. In his ministry, he progressively conquered death. First with Jairus' daughter who was recently declared dead by her relatives (Luke 8:49 – 56). Next with the widow of Nain's son. His body was being carried to his grave when Jesus raised him back to life (Luke 7:11 – 17). Finally, Jesus called life back into Lazarus. He was raised from his tomb after being dead 4 days (John 11:1 – 44). As mentioned earlier, Heaven and the Cosmos were witnesses to these events. Jesus knew he had authority over death.

In obedience to God's plans and will, Jesus submitted himself to the process of crucifixion. The prophecies recorded in Isaiah 53 and the Psalm 22 told Jesus what to expect. By fulfilling these prophecies, his blood would carry the authority and power to overcome death and return humanity to the right relationship to God. His blood would restore humanity to its original purpose in the Cosmos. The first section of Isaiah 53 was already unfolding as recorded in verse 4:

*Surely, He has borne our griefs and carried our sorrows; Yet we esteemed Him stricken, Smitten by God, and afflicted.*

In the exchange with the disciples, Jesus was carrying the griefs and sorrows of all humanity. In fact, he became our sin.

Much has been written in Christian books and recorded in Christian movies about the events from Gethsemane through Jesus' death on the cross and resurrection. It is depicted in a manner that our physical senses and human understanding can grasp the magnitude of the cost Jesus paid as the Lamb of God. The next section reviews the same events from a spiritual viewpoint. The battle Jesus fought in his soul and spirit can be traced by the words he said and the alignment of the physical events with the prophecies in the Bible. Take a moment and pray this scripture to give the reader discernment through the Holy Spirit of these events. As you read it out loud, personalize the prayer. Substitute "me" and "I" for "you" when appropriate. Ephesians 1:17 – 20

*[17]That the God of our Lord Jesus Christ, the Father of glory, may give to you the **spirit of wisdom and revelation in the knowledge of Him**, [18]__the eyes of your understanding__ being enlightened…*

*That you may know what the hope of His calling is. What are the riches of the glory of His inheritance in the saints, [19]and what is the exceeding greatness of **His power toward us who believe**, according to the working of His mighty power*

*[20]Which He worked in Christ when He raised Him from the dead and seated Him at His right hand in the heavenly places,*

Additionally, ask the Holy Spirit to lead you spirit to spirit through these eyes of understanding, overcoming man's wisdom (1 Corinthians 2:12).

Jesus' battle on the cross subjugated all rebellion and its product, sin and chaos under the authority of God. Remember when God created the Cosmos, he gave the blood authority and the power of life. This eternal life is spiritual as well as animating the physical body. As stated in Leviticus 17:11

## 3: Victories of Jesus

> *For the life of the flesh is in the blood, and I have given it to you upon the altar to make atonement for your souls. For it is the blood that makes atonement for the soul.*

As Jesus was bleeding on the cross, he was spiritually directing his blood to subjugate the power in the choice of rebellion to the voice of his blood. He was bending his blood to "kaphar" any power within rebellion that negates the will of God. "Kaphar" is the Jewish word for atonement. Its multilayer meaning is to cover, purge, reconcile, cleanse, and pardon. The fruit of the Tree of Knowledge of Good and Evil was being placed under the authority of the blood of Jesus. He was making atonement for Adam's choice. As recorded in Romans 5:18 - 19

> *[18]Therefore, as through one man's offense judgment came to all men, resulting in condemnation, even so through one Man's righteous act the gift came to all men, resulting in justification of life. [19]For as by one man's disobedience many were made sinners, so also by one Man's obedience many will be made righteous.*

A spiritual exchange was occurring and being witnessed and recorded in the Heavenly Realm. In this spiritual battle between Jesus and Satan, Jesus had faith in the prophecy of Isaiah chapter 53. He knew what it would cost and what he was required to do. As Recorded in Isaiah 53: 5-6

> *[5]But He was wounded for our transgressions; He was bruised for our iniquities… The chastisement for our peace was upon Him, and by **His stripes we are healed.** [6]All we like sheep have gone astray; We have turned, everyone, to his own way; and **the LORD has laid on Him the iniquity of us all.***

With each breath Jesus took, pushing up with his feet and then hanging on with the strength in his arms, he fought. Jesus directed his blood to overcome the power in our iniquities. The blood that was being poured out covered the iniquities we choose to embrace outside the will of our Creator God. Iniquity is translated from the Hebrew word "avon". "Avon" has multiple layers of meaning. They are perversity, moral evil, mischief, sin, and fault. Every action and imagination humanity embraces in rebellion to the will of God was now being placed under the authority and power of the blood of Jesus.

Satan's attack to stop the draining of his power within the souls of humanity was also on multiple spiritual levels. As recorded in Psalm 22:7 - 8

> $^7$*All those who see Me ridicule Me. They shoot out the lip, they shake the head, saying, $^8$"He trusted in the LORD, let Him rescue Him; Let Him deliver Him, since He delights in Him!"*

Mockery, disrespect, and insults were sent to build a sense of failure and isolation. His whole ministerial work was belittled and insulted. These actions are verified in Matthew 27:39 – 42. This noisy clamor was to distract Jesus' concentration. With spiritual eyes Jesus saw demonic spirits sent to pull his spirit and soul from his physical body and hurry the death process before completing the overtaking of every iniquity and transgression with his blood. Psalm 22: 12 – 13

> $^{12}$*Many bulls have surrounded Me; strong bulls of Bashan have encircled Me. $^{13}$They gape at Me with their mouths like a raging and roaring lion.*

This struggle with the strong spiritual demons is also recorded in Matthew 27:45-46. The Cosmos, witness to these spiritual events, reflects the intensity of the battle in the darkness.

The battle intensified. Between the sixth hour and the ninth hour of the day, the Cosmos began to reflect this spiritual battle. All four gospels record this fact. As stated in Mark 15:33 - 34

> $^{33}$*Now when the sixth hour had come there was darkness over the whole land until the ninth hour. $^{34}$And at the ninth hour Jesus cried out with a loud voice, saying, "Eloi, Eloi, lama sabachthani?" which is translated, 'My God, My God, why have You forsaken Me?'*

Jesus uses scripture to align himself and his actions with the will of God. His words are the beginning of Psalm 22. He brings the living spiritual light of the word into the physical world. As Jesus stated to his disciples, he was binding the spiritual life-giving word in earth so his actions would be bound in Heavenly Realms (Matthew 18:18). The success of Jesus battle is recorded in in Luke 23:44 – 46

> *⁴⁴Now it was about the sixth hour, and there was darkness over all the earth until the ninth hour. ⁴⁵Then the sun darkened, and the veil of the temple was torn in two. ⁴⁶And when Jesus cried out with a loud voice, He said,* ***"Father, into Your hands I commit My spirit." Having said this, He breathed His last.***

Jesus won the battle by determining when his spirit and soul would leave his physical body. He declared it to be given unto Father God. Matthew gives more details concerning the response of the Cosmos to the overcoming of the power of the Tree of Knowledge of Good and Evil as noted in Matthew 27:52 – 53

> *⁵¹Then, behold, the veil of the temple was torn in two from top to bottom. The earth quaked, and the rocks were split. ⁵²The graves were opened; and many bodies of the saints who had fallen asleep were raised; ⁵³and* ***coming out of the graves after His resurrection****, they went into the holy city and appeared to many.*

The actions of the Cosmos in the earth and the heavens were reflections of the intensity of the battle between Jesus and Satan in the Spiritual Realm. Victory for Jesus is recorded in his own words where he committed his spirit to Father God as he chose when to release it from his physical body. No person took his life. He surrendered his spirit and soul to God. We also have further evidence of Jesus' victory with his own words. John notes in John 19:30

> *So, when Jesus received the sour wine, He said, "It is finished!" And bowing His head, He gave up His spirit.*

The battle was over. Jesus had taken every drop of his blood and used its power to overcome the power of the seed and fruit of the Tree of Knowledge of Good and Evil in the souls of humanity.

Now a soldier completes the destruction of the power of the curse on the land. In Genesis 3:17 - 18 the consequences of Adam's rebellion are dictated to Adam and his future generations.

> *[17] Then to Adam He said, "Because you have heeded the voice of your wife, and have eaten from the tree of which I commanded you, saying, 'You shall not eat of it': **Cursed is the ground for your sake...***
>
> *In toil you shall eat of it All the days of your life. [18] Both thorns and thistles it shall bring forth for you, and you shall eat the herb of the field."*

Jesus' actions of using his blood to subjugate all the products of rebellion is now applied to the ground. The authority and power in his blood overcomes all curses (Galatians 3:13 – 14). Restoration of the land is achieved when a man pierces Jesus side. As noted in John 19:33 – 35

> *[33] But when they came to Jesus and saw that He was already dead, they did not break His legs. [34] But one of the soldiers pierced His side with a spear, and immediately blood and water came out. [35] And he who has seen has testified, and his testimony is true; and he knows that he is telling the truth, so that you may believe.*

Medical science claims, based on the evidence, Jesus' heart was pierced. The complete draining of any residual blood in Jesus' physical body followed. It was poured into the land. The promise of restoring all within the Cosmos and reconciling it to the intent of its creation was being planted by the blood in the soil.

The action of piercing Jesus' side also aligned with the directions of the first Passover Lamb. All spiritual requirements were to be met. Remember, Jesus is the complete replacement for the animal sacrifices. As noted in the original instructions in Exodus 12:46

> *"In one house it shall be eaten; you shall not carry any of the flesh outside the house, **nor shall you break one of its bones**.*

Just as the death angel passed over the homes of those who obeyed and trusted the words of God, now with the perfect sacrifice of Jesus, death has no power over the blood of Jesus. By completing the pattern of the first Passover lambs, through faith and obedience to God's word the benefit of

## 3: Victories of Jesus

overcoming death is transferred to the victory of Jesus' blood. This is why in Isaiah 53 it is noted, "by his stripes we are healed."

Jesus' physical body has been offered as the final Passover sacrifice. As prophesied in Isaiah 53 and Psalm 22, all requirements have been met. Two witnesses, Heavenly Realms and the Cosmos now testify in the Courts of Heaven to the authenticity of Jesus' actions. God established in the Heavenly Realm a requirement of two witnesses. He gave the same statute to humanity as recorded in Deuteronomy 19:15

> *One witness shall not rise against a man concerning any iniquity or any sin that he commits; by the mouth of two or three witnesses the matter shall be established.*

For all eternity, now the blood of Jesus not only has the power, but also the authority to overcome all iniquities and transgressions bound to the soul of humanity. It is recorded in the Courts of Heaven. This is the final authority to enforce the Justice of Yahweh. The blood also has the authority to overcome death, and its precursor sickness. A covenant with those who in faith accept the body and blood of Jesus in exchange for their own transgressions and iniquities allows them to benefit from the authority and power of Jesus' blood. This is also ordained in the Courts of Heaven. Through the next events, the conditions and benefits of the Blood Covenant of Jesus will be established in Heavenly Realms and the created Cosmos.

Jesus did not stop with these events in his determination to reconcile humanity to its original relationship with God. His spirit body and soul body continue in their spiritual journey to reconcile everything trafficked through Adam in rebellion to the will of God. As noted in Colossians 1:19 - 20

> *[19] For it pleased the Father that in Him all the fullness should dwell. [20] And by Him to reconcile all things to Himself, by Him, **whether things on earth or things in heaven**, having made peace through the blood of His cross.*

Free of his physical body, now the spirit-body and soul-body of Jesus travels the pathway of all humanity takes upon death. There are more victories to achieve. There is a stolen mantle to recover. In these victories, Jesus develops a pathway for all humanity to follow to enter the Kingdom of God. Jesus becomes the Way, the Truth and the Light through these next victories (John 14:6).

# 4

# From Physical Death to Resurrection

Jesus Christ is fully son of man and son of God. As stated in Colossians 2: 9 - 10

> *⁹For in Him dwells all the fullness of the Godhead bodily; ¹⁰and you are complete in Him, who is the head of all principality and power.*

Also as noted in Hebrews 2:17 – 18

> *¹⁷Therefore, in all things He had to be made like His brethren, that He might be a merciful and faithful High Priest in things pertaining to God. And to make propitiation for the sins of the people. ¹⁸For in that He Himself has suffered, being tempted, He is able to aid those who are tempted.*

God ordained humanity would live in our Cosmos in a physical body and then die once (Hebrews 9:27). As noted in an earlier chapter, what choices each person makes, the actions, and attitudes of the heart are recorded in Heavenly Realms. Paul describes this for those alive after Jesus Christ's resurrection in 2 Corinthians 5:10

> *For we must all appear before the judgment seat of Christ, that each one may receive the things done in the body, according to what he has done, whether good or bad.*

The actions in the spiritual realms Jesus accomplished are the victories that underscore the promises for those who submit their will in faith to Jesus Christ as their Lord. Being fully man, now Jesus, who surrendered his soul and spirit to Father God, enters the pathway all follow upon physical death.

While on the cross, Jesus spoke with the thief who addressed him. As recorded in Luke 23, Jesus declares his destiny after his physical death, is Paradise. As recorded in Luke 23:39 – 43

> *[39]Then one of the criminals who were hanged blasphemed Him, saying, "If You are the Christ, save Yourself and us."*
>
> *[40]But the other, answering, rebuked him, saying, "Do you not even fear God, seeing you are under the same condemnation? [41]And we indeed justly, for we receive the due reward of our deeds; but this Man has done nothing wrong."*
>
> *[42]Then he said to Jesus, "Lord, remember me when You come into **Your kingdom**."*
>
> *[43]And Jesus said to him, "Assuredly, I say to you, **today** you will be with Me **in Paradise**."*

In his last moments of life, this thief declared he feared God. Scriptures state this is the beginning of spiritual wisdom (Paslm 111:10). He recognized his actions were against God. He acknowledges he earned his place on the cross. This is a confession to God. He asks for God's grace when Jesus enters his Spiritual Kingdom. The thief states he cannot earn this gift, admitting by his own merits he has no right to it. Yet with a heart filled with repentance, he asks for eternal life, rather than saving his physical life. Grace is granted when Jesus states, "today you will be with me in Paradise". The pattern and actions of a dying man are recorded and witnessed in both Heaven Realms and our Cosmos. Confession, repentance, and asking in faith for grace opens a doorway through Jesus Christ's authority to eternal life.

## Jesus Enters Paradise

Scripture explains what Paradise is. The first mention of Paradise is in Genesis. It is recognized as a possession of Abraham. Jewish tradition interchanges the name, Abraham's Bosom with Paradise. As recorded in Genesis 14: 18 - 19

> *[18]Then Melchizedek king of Salem brought out bread and wine; he was the priest of God Most High. [19]And he blessed him and said:*

> *"Blessed be Abram of God Most High, **Possessor of heaven and earth**; [20]And blessed be God Most High, who has delivered your enemies into your hand." And he gave him a tithe of all.*

In an act of worship, Melchizedek acknowledges Abram has spiritual property in Heaven. The word "possessor" is translated from the Hebrew word "qanah". Its multilayer meaning is to create, to procure or purchase. God promised Abraham a land of which God would reveal to him, if Abram would leave all he had and follow God's directions (Genesis 12:1). The high priest of God declared this truth when releasing a blessing from Heavenly Realms. God has given Abraham spiritual territory in Heaven and on the earth.

Jesus mentions Abraham's Bosom in one of his parables. As recorded in Luke 16:22 – 26

> [22]*"So it was that the beggar died and was carried by the angels to **Abraham's bosom**. The rich man also died and was buried.* [23]*"And being in torments in Hades, he lifted his eyes and **saw Abraham afar off, and Lazarus in his bosom**.* [24]*"Then he cried, saying, 'Father Abraham, have mercy on me; send Lazarus that he may dip the tip of his finger in water and cool my tongue. For I am tormented in this flame.'*
>
> [25]*"But Abraham said, 'Son, remember that in your lifetime you received your good things, and likewise Lazarus evil things; but now he is comforted, and you are tormented.*
>
> [26]*'And besides all this, between us and you there is a great gulf fixed, so that those who want to pass from here to you cannot, nor can those from there pass to us.'*

There are two different places in the spiritual realm that those who die to enter. Abraham's Bosom, or Paradise is set aside for the righteous. God judges a person based on what has been recorded in their book of Life in Heavenly Realms (Hebrews 10:30 – 31 7 Paslm 75:7). Jesus is telling the people, those who received evil in their life, may enter Paradise depending on their heart's intent. God's mercy and grace weighs all things of the heart of everyone when releasing his verdict. With the thief on the cross, Jesus also demonstrated he had the authority to offer grace.

Upon the separation of Jesus' soul and spirit bodies from his physical body, his heart and life were also judged. Thus, as he stated he entered Paradise, or Abraham's Bosom. Here Jesus preached the gospel of the Kingdom of God to those who were judged righteous upon their physical death. Psalm 22 prophesied Jesus would do this as recorded in Psalm 22: 22 – 24

> *[22]I will declare Your name to My brethren; In the midst of the assembly, I will praise You. [23]You who fear the LORD, praise Him All you descendants of Jacob, glorify Him, and fear Him, all you offspring of Israel!*

Those deemed righteous by God were the brethren who heard the Gospel Jesus preached. Jesus explained what he would do when he was teaching his disciples. As recorded in John 5:21 – 25

> *[21]"For as the Father raises the dead and gives life to them, even so the Son gives life to whom He will.*

In his time in Paradise, Jesus enacted the rest of what he said to his disciples as recorded in John 5:24 – 25

> *[24]"Most assuredly, I say to you, he who hears My word and believes in Him who sent Me has everlasting life, and shall not come into judgment, but has passed from death into life. [25]Most assuredly, I say to you, the hour is coming, and now is, when the dead will hear the voice of the Son of God; and those who hear will live.*

Under the new covenant of the Blood of Jesus, righteous standing with God is obtained in exchange for all that was achieved while living under bondage of the Tree of Knowledge of Good and Evil. As noted by Peter in 1 Peter 2: 24 – 25

> *[24]Who Himself bore our sins in His own body on the tree, that we, having died to sins, might live for righteousness— by whose stripes you were healed. [25]For you were like sheep going astray but have now returned to the Shepherd and Overseer of your souls.*

Those deemed righteous by Father God's judgment still needed the victory of the Blood of Jesus to overcome all products of sin in their souls. Even the righteous acts of each person are to be surrendered to the King of Resurrection and Glory, Jesus Christ. Jesus was to be declared by each one to be the Lord over their souls. For he is the way, the truth and the life into the presence of Father God (John 14:6). Now righteousness is defined by entering the new covenant that was prophesied by Jeremiah (31:33 – 34). Jesus declared his words describing his actions and offering the Covenant of the Blood of Jesus to those who occupied Paradise. They became the first to receive the blessings of the Blood of Jesus. The words of scripture were being fulfilled. Jesus was reconciling all those who lived before the Blood of Covenant of Jesus with the new covenant.

As noted earlier, patterns were being witnessed and recorded in the Courts of Heaven. The courts were stamping the authority of the Spiritual Realms to be active in the Cosmos as they are in the eternal Spiritual Realms. Two important patterns with the authority of God behind them were created in Paradise.

1. Confession with our mouths, a faith in our hearts, of Jesus Christ as Lord places each of us under the Blood Covenant of Jesus Christ. We exchange our own righteousness under the old covenant, for the righteousness of Jesus Christ in the new covenant. Then we submit and walk in alignment with this covenant. Romans 10: 8 -10 was established for eternity:

*$^8$But what does it say? "The word is near you, in your mouth and in your heart" (that is, the word of faith which we preach): $^9$that if you confess with your mouth the Lord Jesus and believe in your heart that God has raised Him from the dead, you will be saved. $^{10}$For with the **heart one believes unto righteousness**, and with the mouth **confession is made unto salvation**.*

2. The opportunity for those not conscious in their physical body, as in medical coma, exists for them to hear the Gospel of the Kingdom of God. Just as those in Paradise were not in their physical body and their consciousness rested within, now others in such a state,

before physical death, can hear in their souls the Gospel of God. We may apply this grace to medically unconscious people knowing on a spiritual level they may hear the truth. The center for our wills is in our soul bodies. Choices to accept Jesus Christ can happen.

God's authority and power is not limited. Human understanding is less than the eternal spiritual truth. God's authority is not limited by human's understanding. Faith is the key to entering the Spiritual Realm.

His word is true and will always produce the results he plans (Isaiah 46:10). The victory of Jesus in Paradise, as stated in Isaiah 53:11- 12 is now alive in both the Heavenly Realm and the Cosmos.

> *[11]He shall see the labor of His soul and be satisfied. By His knowledge, my righteous Servant shall justify many; For He shall bear their iniquities. [12]Therefore, I will divide Him a portion with the great. And* **He shall divide the spoil with the strong,** *because He poured out His soul unto death. And He was numbered with the transgressors, And He bore the sin of many, and made intercession for the transgressors.*

## *Jesus Enters Hades*

As Jesus explained to his disciples in the parable recorded in Luke 16:19 – 30, there are two different places the spirit body and soul body of every individual may be sent. It is the judgment of God as to which place the person has earned the right to enter (Hebrews 10:30 – 31). On this side of the cross of Jesus, our faith and the grace of God has given people a method to overcome the iniquities and transgressions that leads to entering Hades.

Jesus told his disciples he would not only die but also return from the dead. In one of those discussions with the Pharisees, Jesus prophesized part of his mission after his physical death and before his resurrection. As recorded in Matthew 12:40

> *"For as Jonah was three days and three nights in the belly of the great fish, so will the Son of Man be three days and three nights in the heart of the earth.*

## 4: From Physical Death to Resurrection

The heart of the earth is not Paradise. In Isaiah 53:9 more clues are given to where this is.

*And they made His grave with the wicked— But with the rich at His death, Because He had done no violence, nor was any deceit in His mouth.*

The wicked were not in Paradise. Their place after death, or in the grave is Hades. In the parable described in Luke 16:19 – 30, a rich man earned a grave in Hades. To complete the mission God gave Jesus for total reconciliation of humanity to its original relationship with God, Jesus was to confront the fallen Lucifer, Satan, in the heart of the earth. As Jesus stated, recorded in John 6:38 – 39

*[38] For I have come down from heaven, not to do My own will, but the will of Him who sent Me. [39]This is the will of the Father who sent Me, that of all He has given Me I should lose nothing but should raise it up at the last day.*

The last day is referring to the third day, his resurrection day. Jesus' mission in entering Hades was to recover all that was trafficked by Adam with Satan. In the covenant with Satan, an exchange happened. The mantle that covered and protected Adam from evil was removed.

Remember Jesus declared no one would take his life. He has the power to lay it down and take it up. So far, his victories have given him

- ➢ authority over the voice of the enemy.
- ➢ authority over the legal power of every agreement made outside of the covenant with God. The power and authority to break this agreement.
- ➢ the authority to bestow eternal life to the righteous dead.

Authority is greater than simply power. Power gives the ability to enact and complete something. Authority in the legal rights, backed by the original source of life, the Heavenly Realms, to overcome all lawlessness and its products. Jesus is operating in these authorities. No man has ever been so united with God and surrendered completely to the will of God. The chasm mentioned Luke 16:19 – 30 is not a barrier to this authority Jesus carries within his soul and spirit bodies. He crosses over into Hades.

To understand what Jesus is seeking, let us return to Genesis chapters two and three. God warned Adam that the consequences of disobedience would activate death (Genesis 2:17). Death and the entity sin are not the beginning of the problem. They are the consequence or result of rebellion against God and his divine order. Too many times, the modern church has focused on the results of rebellion. Until the source, rebellion is recognized, believers in Jesus as Lord are refighting battles already won by King Jesus. To gain authority over the consequences of rebellion requires confrontation. As noted, Jesus' blood now contains the power and the authority to overrule the voice and actions of sin and its final outcome physical death. Corruption in the soul was possible by eating the fruit of the Tree of Knowledge of Good and Evil. By becoming the last lamb of Passover, Jesus has victory over this process. Jesus' blood is imbued with the spiritual authority to overcome the power of every seed of the Tree of Knowledge of Good and Evil. Now Jesus confronts Satan and his demons to take back the spoils of his alternative covenant.

An exchange was enacted between Satan and Adam. An alternative covenant between Satan and Adam was presented to Adam. Satan promised greater wisdom, by knowing good and evil, if Adam would break covenant with God. Adam's actions sealed his participation in this alternative covenant. It could be called the Covenant of Fear and Death. Adam had a choice to trust God and obey his commands or follow another spiritual voice to obtain a promised greater wisdom. Adam allowed Eve to experience the results and complete the action before he participated. Look at what Satan promised as recorded in Genesis 3:4 – 5

> *⁴Then the serpent said to the woman, "You will not surely die.*
> *⁵"For God knows that in the day you eat of it your eyes will be opened, and you will be like God, knowing good and evil."*

The temptation was to become like God, without God's direction and discipline guiding them. A promised shortcut to power and wisdom through opening spiritual eyes was offered. This spiritual power was outside of the harmony and balance within the Cosmos. It could not maintain life. This power can only destroy. They were already children of God. Adam understood what was being offered. He did not see through his spiritual eyes the cost. Adam did not understand the consequences. Death was not a reality in our Cosmos at this time. As God said to Cain, this power would rule over his will and make him a slave (Genesis 4:7). At issue is trusting God and learning truth through obedience and submission or take a shortcut with an alternative spiritual power.

The consequences of accepting an alternative covenant happened immediately. As noted in earlier chapters, Adam and Eve became aware they were naked. The spiritual protection against the powers of evil, a mantle, was gone. It was now in the hands of their new master, Satan. Fear grew in the souls of Adam and Eve when they woke up to the absence of the mantle (Genesis 3:10). This prod of fear within the soul now governed them as they learned what evil could now do. They lost their spiritual protection given through their covenant relationship with God. This is what Jesus was entering Hades to obtain and seal within his authority. The power in the soul governed by fear was to be overcome by the power of love in the complete sacrifice Jesus orchestrated. The winner would have authority over the weaker covenant. As noted in 1 John 4:18 - 19

> *$^{18}$There is no fear in love; but **perfect love casts out fear**, because **fear involves torment**. But he who fears has not been made perfect in love. $^{19}$We love Him because He first loved us.*

On a spiritual level, the root of our creation through our triune God was battling the root of the satanic covenant, fear.

Colossians 2:13 – 16 tells of the order in which Jesus accomplished this task.

> *$^{13}$And you, being dead in your trespasses and the uncircumcision of your flesh, He has made alive together with Him. Having forgiven you all trespasses, $^{14}$having wiped out the handwriting of requirements that was against us, which was contrary to us. And He has taken it out of the way, having nailed it to the cross.*

> [15]*Having disarmed principalities and powers, He made a public spectacle of them, triumphing over them in it.*

On the cross, Jesus paid the price as the Lamb and used the power and authority in his sacrifice embodied now in the blood to forgive our trespasses. In the Courts of Heaven, what had been recorded of these trespasses were removed, wiped out and marked paid in full. In Hades, he disarmed the principalities and powers. These are the demons under the authority of Satan. Strong's concordance assigns number G554 to the Greek word for "disarmed". It is "to totally separate or strip from one". Those in Satan's army were stripped of all power given them through Adam's alignment with the Tree of Knowledge of Good and Evil. While Jesus walked the earth, demons recognized Jesus' authority was greater than their power. A man was so riddled with demons he was placed in chains and confined to the graveyard (Matthew 8:27 – 29). The demons within the man's soul declared the authority and power of Jesus was greater than theirs. As noted in Matthew 8:29

> *And suddenly they cried out, saying, "What have we to do with You, Jesus, You Son of God? Have You come here to torment us before the time?"*

With the physical death of Jesus, those in Hades assumed Jesus would be under the same statutes of all humans. Once dead, he would be assigned to a place and no longer torment them. Yet Jesus crossed the chasm no other being could, including them. He was demonstrating a level of power and authority previously only seen in Adam. Though they knew he was the son of God (Luke 4:41), their knowledge did not match what was happening. It is safe to say, the Fear of the Lord (Psalm 33) entered with Jesus when he walked into Hades.

The public spectacle occurred in Hades. "*Deigmatizō*" is the Greek word translated as "making a public spectacle and to make an example". Satan believed he was making a public spectacle when Jesus was on the cross. As mentioned above the battle on the cross was for Jesus to use his blood to obtain the victory over all demonic powers. This also broke the power of the agreement with the Tree of Knowledge of Good and Evil within the souls of people (Hebrews 9:14). The eternal blood of Jesus cleanses our consciousness!

## 4: From Physical Death to Resurrection

In Hades, Jesus turns the tables on Satan, in his own territory. Jesus demonstrated his power and authority over the principalities and powers. As noted in John 1:14, Jesus is full of grace and truth. Jesus is the light that shines in darkness and the darkness cannot overcome it (John1:5). Fear created through deception and darkness was defeated by the Truth, and the Light (I John 3:8). Jesus released the light and truth in him as a weapon against the Covenant of Fear and Death. His power and authority overcame their power. The Bible states, their power is under the feet of Jesus (Ephesians 1:22). His triumph was noted again by the two witnesses, Heavenly Realms and our Cosmos. He now had the spoils of this conflict in his possession.

We see the results of this conflict and Jesus' possession of the spoils in Revelation 1: 17 -18. Apostle John enters a spiritual vision and hears the voice of the resurrected Jesus Christ. He turns and records how Jesus describes himself.

> *[17]And when I saw Him, I fell at His feet as dead. But He laid His right hand on me, saying to me, "Do not be afraid;* ***I am the First and the Last.*** *[18]**I am He who lives, and was dead, and behold, I am alive forevermore. Amen.***
>
> *And I have the keys of Hades and of Death."*

In Jewish understanding keys represent the authority and power over something. Jesus stripped the beings in Hades, the principalities and powers, of their power to overcome the will of a person. He went farther and now had authority even over Satan and his alternative covenant to determine who may enter Hades. The Covenant of the Blood of Jesus has greater authority than this Covenant with Satan. As in the first Passover, Jesus left with the spoils of war. He took back the mantle Adam possessed that sealed humanity from the powers of evil. The results of participation in the covenant with Satan, death, were now under the authority and power of Jesus. Not only is the Key of death in Jesus's possession, but also all the other works of the power of Satan that leads to death. Jesus declared this to his disciples in Matthew 28: 18.

> *And Jesus came and spoke to them, saying, "All authority has been given to Me in heaven and on earth."*

Everything created, all spiritual powers, in both the Cosmos and the Spiritual Realms are now under his authority. Nothing has the ability or power to overrule him. Jesus' legal authority in the Courts of Heaven always overcomes the power of darkness, the enemy wields. As summarized in Colossians 1:13 - 18

> *[13] He has delivered us from the power of darkness and conveyed us into the kingdom of the Son of His love, [14] in whom we have redemption through His blood, the forgiveness of sins.*
>
> *[15] He is the image of the invisible God, the firstborn over all creation. [16] For by Him all things were created that are in heaven and that are on earth, visible and invisible, whether thrones or dominions or principalities or powers. All things were created through Him and for Him.*
>
> *[17] And He is before all things, and in **Him all things consist**.*
>
> *[18] And He is the head of the body, the church, who is the beginning, the firstborn from the dead, that in **all things** He may have the preeminence.*

Jesus is the final arbitrator through his spiritual authority recorded by the victory he had in Hades. Jesus also has total authority over death, the final product of rebellion. As stated in Hebrews 9:15

> *And for this reason, He is the Mediator of the new covenant, by means of death, for the redemption of the transgressions under the first covenant. So that those who are called may receive the promise of the eternal inheritance.*

With these victories in his possession, Jesus has two missions left to accomplish. In these next two victories, Jesus will forge the pathway for others to follow to spiritually enter the presence of God while still in their physical bodies.

## *Jesus returns to His Broken Physical Body*

As noted in earlier chapters, one of Jesus' mission assignments was to create a new pathway for humanity to enter the presence of God. As observed earlier, Jeremiah prophesied this new covenant, and it was quoted in Hebrews (Jeremiah 31:31 -34 & Hebrews 8:7 12). In verse 34 of Jeremiah, clues are given to the new pathway Jesus is creating. Jeremiah 33:34

> *No more shall every man teach his neighbor, and every man his brother, saying, 'Know the LORD'. For they all shall know Me, from the least of them to the greatest of them, says the LORD. For I will forgive their iniquity, and their sin I will remember no more.*

"To know" in Hebrew is "yada'. The multi-layer meaning is to properly see on many levels such as to discern but also to be diligently aware. A personal relationship with God will guide someone in how to function in the new covenant. In the new covenant, the previous mantle of protection is bestowed through an intimate relationship with God. No longer is it achieved as before, through someone teaching another. The mystery of where this mantle resides now in revealed in Jesus' discussion with Nicodemus.

Nicodemus sought spiritual truth from Jesus. It is recorded in John 3:1 – 21. Jesus explains to Nicodemus the method of this new covenant in John 3:5 – 7

> *$^5$Jesus answered, "Most assuredly, I say to you, unless one is born of water and the Spirit, he cannot enter the kingdom of God. $^6$That which is born of the flesh is flesh, and that which is **born of the Spirit is spirit.** $^7$Do not marvel that I said to you, 'You must be born again.'*

Spiritually speaking, being born of water is the baptism that John initiated and Jesus continued. It is a baptism for repentance. As noted in Luke 3:11

> *"I indeed baptize you with water unto repentance, but He who is coming after me is mightier than I, whose sandals I am not worthy to carry. He will baptize you with the **Holy Spirit and fire**.*

The baptism of spirit and fire was the goal of Jesus as he completes these next two missions. As stated in scripture Jesus is the way the truth and the light (John 14:6). We enter the presence of God through him and his righteousness (1 Peter 2:24). In victory Jesus seeks the Holy Spirit to place his soul body and spirit body back into the broken physical body in the tomb or grave. Jesus was first placed in his mother's womb and brooded over by the Holy Spirit. To be born again, the same process of the Holy Spirit bringing him back is necessary to complete the prophecies recorded in Heavenly Realms. He is to be reborn by spirit into a resurrected physical body. Ephesians 1: 19 – 20 describes the two events accomplished through the power of the Spirit.

> *$^{19}$And what is the exceeding greatness of His power toward us? Those who believe,* **according to the working of His mighty power,** *$^{20}$***which He worked in Christ** *when* **He raised Him from the dead and** *seated Him at His right hand in the heavenly places…*

First the Holy Spirit used his power to raise Jesus from the dead in Hades and return him to his broken body.

A mystery is revealed when Holy Spirit again broods over Jesus. One of Holy Spirit's attributes is first revealed to us in Genesis 1:2. He hovered over the waters or brooded like a hen broods over her eggs. When Father God spoke "light be" this brooding united the eternal creative life power with the Word of God. This is the first recorded action of Holy Spirit. He brings creative eternal life to what was chaos and disorder. When he brooded over Mary, he brought the original light of God with its creative eternal life into unity with the egg of Mary to build the body of Jesus. This is the second brooding. When Jesus is baptized at the Jordan, Holy Spirit descends like a dove, again brooding over Jesus. In this third brooding, the power of creative eternal life is bonded into Jesus's soul. Now in this fourth brooding, Holy Spirit uses his creative eternal life-giving power to raise Jesus from Hades to place him into his broken physical body. This brooding also activates new blood.

All of Jesus' blood was drained in his death. The truth is the Hosts of Heaven gathered this spiritual blood that was now imbued with power and authority to reserve to be used later. Holy Spirit created new blood into the broken body of Jesus. Remember the power of life is in the blood. As this new blood is activated and brooded over, resurrection power is called forth. The resurrection power is united with the creative eternal life (living light of Holy Spirit) as Holy Spirit broods over Jesus' broken body. It is implanted in this fourth time blessed blood. Jesus becomes the new creation, the firstborn of the dead. He is filled with resurrection power and authority. Jesus carries resurrection authority in this newly untied three bodies in one. Jesus is truly a new creation. His blood is resurrection blood. As a new creation, this blood has a specific voice with specialized authority and power in both Spiritual Realms and our Cosmos. It has never been tainted with the Tree of Knowledge of Good and Evil.

A pattern is now established and recorded in Heavenly Courts. Jesus is born again by the spark of eternal spiritual life-light. Those who believe and have faith that Jesus is the son of God, who died and was resurrected may participate in this same method of being born again in spirit. As Jesus told Nicodemus, spirit births spirit. Jesus asked Father God in the presence of his disciples for this process. His request was made after the Covenant of the Blood was enacted in the Holy Communion. Though the disciples may not have recognized it then, this was the ultimate goal of the Blood Covenant of Jesus. Jesus prayed with his disciples, recorded in John 17:20 – 24

> *[20]"I do not pray for these alone, but also for those **who will believe in Me through their word**. [21]That they all may be one, as You, **Father, are in Me, and I in You**; that they also may be one in Us, that the world may believe that You sent Me.*
>
> *[22]"And the glory which You gave Me I have given them, that they may be one **just as We are one**.*
>
> *[23]"I in them, and You in Me; that they may be made perfect in one, and that the world may know You have sent Me, and **have loved them as You have loved Me.**"*

The unity of Jesus living in us, through the same power that raised Jesus from the dead (Ephesians 1:19 – 20) is the now a spiritual reality. The prophecy of Jeremiah 33:34, to know God is fulfilled. We know him intimately when he lives in us in the rebirth of our spirit. The mantle of protection Adam carried has become a living presence inside the soul/spirit bodies of the believer. As Jeremiah stated, we are given new hearts as we walk out the pathway Jesus has created. Our minds are renewed when we follow Jesus' pattern of covering every thought and emotions with the word of God (2 Corinthians 10:5). When we live in the Covenant of the Blood of Jesus, our wills are surrendered to God in obedience. The Holy Spirit will teach us how to accomplish this as Jesus declared in John 16:12 -15.

When the curtain of the tabernacle was torn from top to bottom (Mark 15:38) Father God was announcing what separated every individual from his holiness was now open in a new way. Jesus' victories become the stones in this new pathway to now enter the presence of God. He is our solid rock, or foundation to new life (Isaiah 28:16). His righteousness covers the believer (Ephesians 6:14). The renewed, reborn spirit of Jesus within the believer allows each person access to the throne of God. As recorded in Hebrews 10:19 - 22

> *[19]Therefore, brethren, having boldness to enter the Holiest by the blood of Jesus, [20]by a new and living way which He **consecrated for us, through the veil, that is, His flesh**,*
>
> *[21]and having a High Priest over the house of God, [22]let us draw near with a **true heart in full assurance of faith**. And having our hearts sprinkled from an evil conscience and our bodies washed with pure water.*

By faith, through our confession and willing submission to our Lord and savior Jesus Christ all may now enter the presence of our God.

## Completing the Cycle

One assignment was left for Jesus to complete. The second part of Ephesians 1:20 happened next. The power of the Holy Spirit raises Jesus to enter the Heavenly Realms. Here, Jesus completes what is noted in Ephesians 1:21 – 23

> *[21]Far above **all principality and power and might and dominion**, and every name that is named, not only in this age but also in that which is to come. [22]And **He put all things under His feet** and gave*

## 4: From Physical Death to Resurrection

*Him to be head over all things to the church, $^{23}$which is His body, the fullness of Him who fills all in all.*

Jesus enters the Heavenly Realms. He enters as the high priest of the order of Melchizedek (Hebrews 5:5 -6). The tabernacle that Moses commissioned was a physical copy of the eternal tabernacle in the Holies of Holies of Heaven. Jesus enters the eternal tabernacle to make his offering once for all humanity. As recorded in Hebrews 9:11

*$^{11}$But Christ came as High Priest of the good things to come, with the greater and more perfect tabernacle not made with hands, that is, not of this creation. $^{12}$Not with the blood of goats and calves, but with His own blood He entered the Most Holy Place once for all, having obtained eternal redemption.*

Jesus pours his spiritual blood, that was collected by the Host of Heaven, onto the mercy seat. As recorded in Hebrews 10:12 – 14

*$^{12}$But this Man, after He offered one sacrifice for sins forever, sat down at the right hand of God, $^{13}$from that time waiting till His enemies are made His footstool. $^{14}$For by one offering He has perfected forever those who are being sanctified.*

In this action, a cycle is completed in accordance with the statutes in Heavenly Realms. What began at the first Passover, repeated each Jewish year by the believers, and foreshadowed with Abraham and Isaac on Mount Moriah, were now completed in Heavenly Realms at the eternal tabernacle. The laws and statutes that formed the Cosmos are maintained.

As Jesus taught his disciples, God gave humanity dominion over his creation, the Cosmos (Genesis 1:28 -30). In this gift came the responsibility to occupy and possess it as it is in Heavenly Realms. The beginning of the Lord's Prayer (Luke 11:1 – 4) declares this truth.

*Your kingdom Come. Your will be done on earth as it is in heaven.*

We, his creation, are declaring our allegiance to our Creator. We are announcing to the Cosmos our willingness to subjugate our actions under God's will.

Jesus further told his disciples as recorded in Matthew 16: 19

> *And I will give you the keys of the kingdom of heaven, and whatever you bind on earth will be bound in heaven, and whatever you loose on earth will be loosed in heaven.*

The Greek word for binding, means to put under legal obligation. As noted earlier, keys represent authority. These are used to invoke the spiritual authority of Heavenly Courts and enforce their authority over lawlessness. As a man and a new creation, Jesus Christ is representing all people as he enters the Holy Tabernacle of God. He enacts a sacred duty to put into agreement what he did, his victories under the authority of Heavenly Courts. His victories are bound in Heaven as they were bound on Earth. This releases dominion into his hands. All that was legally taken under the alternative covenant with Satan is eternally broken through Jesus Christ, the new creation. Dominion is even greater than authority. Webster's dictionary defines "dominion" as the right to control, direct and use. It also means supreme authority to govern. In this final act of Jesus as both a newly created man and high priest of the order Melchizedek, all rights, authority and power are under the feet of Jesus. He has dominion over all!

As mentioned earlier, Matthew recorded Jesus announcing all power and authority was given to him in heaven and earth (Matthew 28:18). This is added to what Mark recorded concerning the return of dominion to the head of the church, Jesus Christ. Mark 16:15 -18

> *[15] And He said to them, "Go into all the world and preach the gospel to every creature. [16] He who believes and is baptized will be saved; but he who does not believe will be condemned.*
>
> *[17] And these signs will follow those who believe: In My name they will cast out demons. They will speak with new tongues; [18] they will take up serpents; and if they drink anything deadly, it will by no means hurt them; they will lay hands on the sick, and they will recover."*

The power, authority, and dominion are given to those who believe and make Jesus Christ their Lord. We are to enforce the victories of Jesus as we submit under his authority. These covenant blessings are to flow through us, his church. As Jesus lives in our souls, we become one with all he is. We abide in Jesus, and he abides in us (Ephesians 3: 17). It is in faith, surrender, trust, obedience, and humility we return to our destiny as children of God. Let us follow the leadings of the Holy Spirit to sanctify ourselves, as ordained by Jesus. Let us rise in faith and follow the complete pathway of victories forged by our King and Lord, Jesus Christ. It is not a battle over the power of the enemy but rather enforcing what is already won! We are to call the truth as it is recorded in Heavenly Courts into our lives and regions. Lawlessness, lies, and deceptions of the enemy cannot stand in the light of truth. We are the light bearers, the truth-talkers, and the enforcers of the righteousness of our King and Master, Jesus Christ. So let us go boldly into our Cosmos declaring the living word of God!

*Diane M. Neuman*

# 5

# Applying the Blood

One of the many spiritual attributes of our Lord and King Jesus Christ is he is the vine. As the spiritual vine, we abide in him, he abides in us. Jesus declares this truth as noted in John 15:5

*I am the vine; you are the branches. He who abides in Me, and* ***I in him****, bears much fruit;* ***for without Me you can do nothing.***

The fruit is spiritual fruit. It is Jesus' righteousness we have received in the Covenant of the Blood of Jesus that allows us to live in this reality. This is why it is stated, "without Me you can do nothing." These truths are recorded in Heavenly Realms. We who have submitted ourselves to the Covenant of the Blood of Jesus are under his authority. It is an act of faith, daily renewed as we seek Jesus' will in our lives. Jesus further explains in verse 10 of the same chapter how this is accomplished.

*If you keep My commandments,* ***you will abide in My love****, just as I have kept My Father's commandments and abide in His love.*

As the vine he nourishes us. As a branch, we bring his truth and light into our Cosmos. We participate in the beginning of the Lord's Prayer, that the will of God be done on earth as it is in heaven. This unity is a giving of love and gratitude to Jesus for who he is. As Jesus states in John 14:15

*If you love Me, keep My commandments.*

As mentioned in earlier chapters, love is the power behind the work of Jesus and his victories. Love is both a power and a spiritual substance. Like faith, it is eternal. Our God is love (1 John 4:16). It is when we participate in love and seek God above all else, we activate the authority of the Covenant of the Blood of Jesus over the Covenant of Fear and Death. We abide in Jesus and follow his pattern of surrendering our will as an offering of gratitude and love. The love enables us to let go of our old ways and enter into a new life. Our actions follow from united love.

The Covenant of the Blood of Jesus is a covenant established in eternal living love. This love is what defeated the darker covenant empowered through fear. As we seek Jesus, we are to sanctify ourselves through the blood of Jesus (John17:19). As noted in Galatians 2:20

> *I have been crucified with Christ. It is no longer I who live, but **Christ lives in me**. And the life which I now live in the flesh **I live by faith in the Son of God**, who **loved me** and gave Himself for me.*

We are connected to the vine, our source of new life through love. Our love response feeds and nourishes the eternal living love as we abide in Jesus Christ. Obedience is the outcome of love. Jesus, the truth and the light of the world shines in our souls, overcoming all darkness. In submission to the covenant of the Blood of Jesus, we continually die to our old self and become one with Jesus. It is a process. The living spiritual blood of Jesus flowing through the vine enables this process.

Our triune God is eternal. Though his thoughts are not our thoughts, and his ways greater than our ways (Isaiah 55:9), we learn to know him through his attributes. As God revealed himself through his actions we became better acquainted with him. Some examples are

- ➤ El Shaddai: Genesis 17: 1- 21 (God all mighty)
- ➤ Yahweh-Jirah: Genesis 22:14 (God who provides)
- ➤ Yahweh-Raphe: Exodus 15: 22 – 26 (God who heals)
- ➤ Yahweh-Nissi: Exodus 1:15 (God who is our banner)

In each situation, his nature was shown to his people. When we approach God, and call on these specific names, we bring attention to the specific promises God's names invoke. We remember and ask God to do again what he did before as recorded in the Bible. We ask for the same results in our situations. As noted in 2 Timothy 3:16 - 17

> *[16] All Scripture is given by inspiration of God, and is profitable for doctrine, for reproof, for correction, for instruction in righteousness, [17] that the man of God may be complete, thoroughly equipped for every good work.*

This spiritual reality is also true for the spiritual eternal blood of Jesus. The next section of this chapter will also attach scriptures to bring into clarity the authority and power of the blood of Jesus. When we apply these scriptures and call in faith for the power and authority of the blood to be released in our specific situations, the victories of Jesus overcomes what we are facing.

## Salvation Blood

In accepting Jesus as Lord of one's life, we enter the Covenant of the Blood of Jesus. It is in our hearts we surrender our old self in exchange for salvation. As stated in Romans 10:9 - 10

> *[9] That if you confess with your mouth **the Lord Jesus** and believe in your heart that God has raised Him from the dead, you will be saved. [10] For with the **heart one believes unto righteousness**, and with the **mouth confession** is made unto salvation.*

Our declaration is recorded in our book of life in Heavenly Realms. We align with Jesus as our Lord. We place ourselves under the Covenant of the Blood of Jesus. This truth, along with Romans 5: 8 – 9 are to be written on our hearts as a guiding light to our rebirth in Jesus.

> *[8] But God demonstrates His own love toward us, in that while we were still sinners, Christ died for us. [9] Much more then, having now been justified by His blood, we shall be saved from wrath through Him.*

We are to remember, God knew us, as we are. Nothing was hidden from his understanding (Hebrews 4:13). We know our failings and hide them from others. Yet, God in love, came to us. He did not require us to clean up our souls before we come into fellowship with God. Instead, God gave us his only son to stand in the gap and pay the price for our transgressions. We are to trust this spiritual truth. Salvation blood cleanses. It breaks the voice of the accuser that we are not worthy, or good enough. It breaks the lies of the voice that keep bringing up our past to ground us into depression, anxiety, and self-rejection. The voice of the Blood of Salvation shatters the voice of condemnation and guilt. Our past rebellion, living our lives on our own terms, rather than submitting to God, is totally forgiven and wiped clean. God has removed it as far as the east is from the west (Psalm 103:12 – 14). Do not allow yourself to hang onto what no longer exists in the Spiritual Realms. Do not re-create it in your thoughts or emotions. The wrath for this rebellion is paid with the Blood of Salvation. We are to apply the Salvation Blood to any critical voice attacking our thoughts, emotions, and memories. Declare the victory of the Blood of Salvation over every thought that is trying to hold you captive (2 Corinthians 5:10).

When we start battling this voice of condemnation and temptation in our minds, we are to remember Jesus in the Garden of Gethsemane. We can call on his victory and declare the voice, power, and authority of the Blood of Salvation defeats the words of the enemy. By returning and reading scriptures of this event, as recorded in the gospels, we bring spiritual truth into our souls. His words are truth and food for our soul. We claim this victory as we surrender our will as Jesus did. The light of truth overcomes the lies of Satan. The battle has already been won. Now stand on the truth of Ephesians 2:8

> *[8]For by grace you have been saved through faith, and that not of yourselves; it is the gift of God, [9]not of works, lest anyone should boast.*

Let go of arguing, defending and trying to prove this victory. Stand in faith and declare the word of God. This sword of the spirit cuts through lies (Hebrews 4:12). When we recognize this is an unearned gift, we can hold the promise and the victory. Sometimes the enemy will change his voice to accuse a person of bragging. When we complete actions for our God, the temptation of owning the work arises. Ephesians 2:9 addresses these thoughts. The temptation of pride is broken through this verse.

The strongest weapon we have against the lies of the enemy, which tries to convince someone they are not a new creation in Christ, is calling on the name of Jesus. By the Blood of Salvation, we have invited Jesus to live within us and occupy our hearts. As Peter preached on Pentecost, salvation comes by calling this truth forward. Acts 2:21

*And it shall come to pass That whoever calls on the name of the LORD Shall be saved.*

Peter is quoting scripture to the people of Jerusalem. God also declared his promise of salvation in Psalms. As noted in Psalm 37:39

*But the salvation of the righteous is from the LORD; He is their strength in the time of trouble.*

Remember, we made Jesus Christ our LORD! This gift, salvation, is ours. As Jesus asked for help in the garden, we ask for the strength of God to come into us. God is faithful. Just as God sent angels to help Jesus, he will send help to those who stand in faith. Declare the spiritual truth. As noted in 1 John 4:4

*You are of God, little children, and **have overcome them**, because **He who is in you** is greater than he who is in the world.*

Finally, remember the enemy is lawless and a liar (John 8:44). Do not expect him to fight fairly. Stand in truth and keep declaring the victories in the blood of Jesus as recorded in the Courts of Heaven. We have dominion through the victories of Jesus. It is not a debate. It is a spiritual fact. We live in grace and truth. Keep repeating and layering your soul with the word and truth of God. As God said to Paul recorded in 2 Corinthians 12:9

*"And He said to me, 'My grace is sufficient for you, for My strength is made perfect in weakness.' Therefore, most gladly I will rather boast in my infirmities, that the power of Christ may rest upon me."*

The voice that accuses focuses on the dead past infirmities. Not by our own strength, power, wisdom, or effort do we overcome. See what the word states as how we are overcomers. Revelation 12:11

*And they overcame him **by the blood of the Lamb and by the word of their testimony**, and they did not love their lives to the death.*

Testify who you are in Christ under the blood covenant. We have already died with Jesus on his cross. Our King has the keys of death, not the enemy. We are members of our King Jesus' Kingdom. We choose not to prioritize the physical life over our eternal spiritual life. The enemy does not define the terms of the battle or the fight. King Jesus Christ does! We his people, declare the truth, live by grace and follow him in faith and love.

## *<u>The Blood of Redemption</u>*

Redemption is achieved through an exchange. It began at the Last Supper, or the Passover meal Jesus shared with his disciples before going to the cross. As noted earlier, he spiritually united his body to theirs, in the new pattern through sharing the bread. A covenant was formed whereby what happened to Jesus' physical body would be exchanged for their iniquities and transgressions. When we remember this exchange and honor it by taking Holy Communion, we are declaring the Covenant of the Blood of Jesus for our life. Spiritually we declare our body is one with Jesus' body. As recorded in Colossians 1:18

> *And* **He is the head of the body**, *the church, who is the beginning, the firstborn from the dead, that in all things He may have the preeminence.*

The first part of activating the power and authority of the Blood of Redemption is renewing this covenant in unity with the body of Jesus Christ. We are to declare and write on our soul the authority of Jesus Christ over our lives. Again, it is recorded in Ephesians 1:22 – 23

> *[22]And He put all things under His feet and gave Him to be head over all things to the church, [23]which is His body, the fullness of Him who fills all in all.*

We align our soul body and spirit body with the truth of belonging to King Jesus. It is an act of faith in surrendering to his authority above anything else. It is recognizing the authority of Spiritual Realm above that of the Cosmos. We are reinstating our choice to obey and submit under the terms of the Covenant of the Blood of Jesus.

The second part of the exchange now can occur. As recorded in Ephesians 1: 7 – 8

> [7]*In Him we have redemption through His blood, the forgiveness of sins, according to the riches of His grace,* [8]*which He made to abound toward us in all wisdom and prudence…*

The truth of power and authority of grace has already been mentioned in an earlier discussion. When it is combined with the statement that it will "abound towards us", Holy Spirit is telling us the living grace moves towards our redeemed spirits. The grace will more than cover our soul body and spirit body. It will overflow through us as it enters our souls. We are to nurture this unity daily. As we seek intimate time with our King Jesus through studying scriptures, prayers, and praise this grace moves into us. This sharing of the living grace will instruct us in all wisdom as known in the Spiritual Realm. We also will gain "prudence". Strong's Concordance numbers this word "5428". It's Greek word, represented by this number means "knowledge and Holy Love of the will of God". The power and authority of the redemptive blood of Jesus exchanges our transgressions, iniquities, and patterns of thinking with Jesus' righteousness. When we operate within this power and authority as we submit to Jesus daily in love and surrender to the will of God, then God's wisdom overcomes all old patterns of thinking. Our greatest desire is to be in the will of God. Our love for God is transformed by our obedience. This desire births actions that become a gift of love. In our private intimate time with Jesus, we can remind him he is the vine, and we are the branch. We can ask that the Blood of Redemption pour from him and cleanse us of anything that does not honor Jesus as our Lord and King.

We enter a deeper covenant through our actions of daily surrendering to God's will. We exchange our old thinking, our own understanding, lack luster tolerance of temptations, and habits of justifying our actions for the righteousness of Jesus. It is done by following the patterns Jesus did when he lived in his physical body. As noted in 2 Timothy 3:16 – 17, we use the living word of God to teach us how to accomplish this task. This lawless being, our enemy, is still trying to live in our souls. We are to enforce the victories of Jesus and place everything in our souls under the authority of the

Blood of Jesus. This is an active war to shut the gates in our soul so only the Holy Love of God lives in us. As noted in 2 Corinthians 10:3 – 5

> *³For though we walk in the flesh, we do not war according to the flesh. ⁴For the weapons of our warfare are not carnal. But mighty in God for pulling down strongholds, ⁵casting down arguments and every high thing that exalts itself against the knowledge of God, bringing every thought into captivity to the obedience of Christ,*

Our weapons are the living eternal truth as given in the living Word of God and the authority and power of the Blood of Jesus. We call the greater authority of Heavenly Realms into our souls through this blood of Redemption. Remember this is done by relying on the Holy Love of the will of God. In seeking God, as we surrender daily to him, we are to develop a love for his will over our own will. The enforcement is a declaration of the spiritual truth using the Word of God, while surrendering to God's will. This builds on the love and gratitude released through the act of abiding in Jesus. Loving God and seeking him continually keeps us in the will of God. For love is an act of giving.

In addition to these truths, we call on the Blood of Redemption to destroy our past habits of the mind. These old thinking habits tend to pop up in times of trial and stress. They were developed without true spiritual wisdom or understanding under the Covenant of Fear and Death. Paul states in 2 Corinthians 10:5 we are to capture every thought. This includes the old pattern of thinking. Jesus relied on scripture to find the patterns that would conquer these habits of the mind. Proverbs 3:5 – 6

> **⁵Trust in the LORD** *with all your heart and* **lean not on your own understanding***;* **⁶***in all your ways acknowledge Him, and He shall* **direct your paths***.*

To overcome self-understanding and wisdom that relies on the five senses we are to not only walk in faith but also trust. Trusting our past experiences as a guide for determining our actions, throws us back into the Tree of Knowledge of Good and Evil. It opens the possibility of unlocking doors in our souls that have been shut through the Blood Covenant of Jesus. In these types of battles, as noted, we are to use spiritual weapons. As stated in Romans 12:2

> *And do not be conformed to this world, but be transformed by the renewing of your mind, that you may prove what is that good and acceptable and **perfect will of God**.*

Seek God's will over your own will. Search the scriptures for the promises in past victories of God over the enemy. The living word of the accounts, such as Pharoah's defeat, Goliath's defeat, or Hannah's prayers for a child, all show patterns of God's hands as he gives victory. As noted earlier, remembering is aligning with the faith they had and calling for God to do it again in your situation. When we align with these living words and trust them above what we might be sensing, thinking, and seeing in our lives, then God can move. Declare the truth of the authority of the Blood of Redemption in acknowledging 1 Corinthians 2:16

> *For "who has known the mind of the LORD that he may instruct Him?" **But we have the mind of Christ.***

Our triune God sent a helper, or counselor to teach us this method and wisdom. As noted earlier, Jesus promised the presence of the Holy Spirit to abide in his disciples. As described in Acts 1:5 Jesus tells them what will happen.

> *"For John truly baptized with water, but you shall be baptized with the Holy Spirit not many days from now."*

This baptism would provide power from the Heavenly Realms (Acts 1:8). Pentecost is honored in the church to remember the event in the upper room. As described in Acts 2:1- 4

> *¹When the Day of Pentecost had fully come; they were all with **one accord in one place**. ²And suddenly there came a **sound from heaven, as of a rushing mighty wind**, and it filled the whole house where they were sitting.*
>
> *³Then there appeared to them **divided tongues, as of fire, and one sat upon each of them**. ⁴And they were **all filled with the Holy***

***Spirit*** *and began to speak with other tongues, as the Spirit gave them utterance.*

The baptism of the Holy Spirit allows him to abide in our souls, just like Jesus does when we actively participate in the Covenant of the Blood of Jesus.

Jesus described the Holy Spirit power in John 16:13 - 14

*$^{13}$"However, when He, the Spirit of truth, has come,* **He will guide you into all truth**. *For He will not speak on His own authority, but whatever He hears He will speak; and He will tell you things to come. $^{14}$"He will glorify Me, for* **He will take of what is Mine and declare it to you.**

The Holy Spirit will convict us of what is truth. He will show us what is hidden in our souls. Through this wisdom, we can go to the Throne of Grace in Heavenly Realms (Hebrews 4:16). With the conviction of the Holy Spirit, we then apply the Blood of Redemption. Here is the pattern:

- ➤ Confess what the Holy Spirit has shown is hiding in your soul
- ➤ Repent of any agreement with this rebellion to the will of God
- ➤ Admit what is in your soul is offensive to God
- ➤ Ask God to forgive you for harboring it
- ➤ Ask Jesus to break any legal right given to what is harboring in your soul by the Authority and Power of the Blood of Redemption
- ➤ Ask Jesus to wipe your book of life with Jesus' Blood of Redemption to erase any memory of what you did that allowed the sin to enter and live in your soul
- ➤ Give praise and Thanksgiving for all that Jesus is

We are applying the scripture from 1 John 1:9 in the process listed above.

*If we confess our sins, He is faithful and just to forgive us our sins and to cleanse us from all unrighteousness.*

We work in tandem with the Blood of Redemption, the Word of God, and the Holy Spirit. Holy Spirit convicts us. We enter the Spiritual Realm not in our own righteousness, rather by the righteousness of King Jesus. We apply the living truth in the Word of God, trusting God is faithful to his Word. As noted in Hebrews 9:15

*For this reason, He is the Mediator of the new covenant. Mediator by means of death,* **for the redemption of the transgressions** *under the first covenant, that those who are called may receive* **the promise of the eternal inheritance**.

By taking these things to the Courts of Heaven, we operate under the dominion and authority God placed in Heavenly Realms over our Cosmos. We declare King Jesus' victory in our souls. God's eternal truths are manifested as we stand in faith and trust, surrendering ourselves in Holy Living love of the will of God.

## The Blood of Reconciliation

God's definition of reconciliation is to bring back into complete unity, harmony, and peace that which was torn asunder. The nature of our creation is upheld in unity with the creator. Our God is the source of life in our Cosmos. There is an active balance, held through spiritual communications between Heavenly Realms and our Cosmos. As mentioned earlier, God spoke his creation into existence. He breathed life into Adam. There is a vibration or sound that accompanies all created things that maintains their existence. It is in harmony with its source, our Creator, planted within it. When God reconciles, he brings what was in disorder and chaotic bondage back to perfect alignment with the original sound and its intent. This is why Jesus taught his disciples to pray, "Thy Kingdom Come, thy will be done, on earth as it is in Heaven."

The blood of reconciliation carries the attributes of this level of reconciliation. As noted in Colossians 1: 19 – 22

> [19]*For it pleased the Father that in Him all the fullness should dwell.* [20]*And by Him to **reconcile all things to Himself, by Him,** whether things on earth or things in heaven, **having made peace through the blood of His cross**.* [21]*And you, who once were alienated and enemies in your mind by wicked works, yet now He has reconciled* [22]*in the body of His flesh through death, to present you holy, and blameless, and above reproach in His sight…*

When we apply the attributes of the Blood of Jesus to our lives we are calling for the power and authority of the Blood to accomplish in our lives all the victories of King Jesus. When we focus on this attribute of the Blood of Reconciliation, we are agreeing with our God to align our lives with His purpose for our lives. We are agreeing to be cleansed and made holy in the sight of our God. We are asking God to stretch our faith, our trust, and our dependency on him. With the attribute of the Blood of Redemption, we developed a holy love for the will of God. Things we formerly tolerated in our souls we took to the Courts of Heaven to be cleansed. Now we are moving closer to God asking for all of our bodies, soul, spirit and physical to be aligned with the harmony and unity of Heavenly Realms. It takes a greater surrender and trust level to submit to the Holiness of God. As noted earlier, the attitude of the Fear of the Lord guides us in the process. Again, the Holy Spirit will teach us all things in how to accomplish applying the attribute of the Blood of Reconciliation.

## Greater harmony with Spiritual Realm

As with all applications within the Covenant of the Blood of Jesus, faith and the Word of God are the methods and clues to enter this process. To better understand faith, we are to look at the life of Abraham, who was called the Father of Faith. As noted in Galatians 3:6

> [6]*Just as Abraham "**believed God, and it was accounted to him for righteousness**."* [7]*Therefore know that only those who are of faith are sons of Abraham.* [8]*And the Scripture, foreseeing that God would justify the Gentiles by faith, preached the gospel to Abraham beforehand, saying, "In you all the nations shall be blessed."* [9]***So then those who are of faith are blessed with believing Abraham.***

What is the level of trust and faith Abraham developed? How deep was the unity and harmony between Abraham and Father God? Over time, these events happened

- Abraham left all that he knew, the land and his people to follow God's promise to a destination only God knew (Genesis 12:5).
- He followed God through unknown territory held by other tribes (Gensis 12:6- 9).
- He gave up the prime land he inhabited to his nephew Lot and God awarded him other lands (Genesis 13:7 – 12).
- He made a covenant with God (Genesis 15:18).
- Abraham and all his people sealed their unity with God through circumcision (Genesis 17).
- God visited Abraham to tell him about his decision for Sodom (Genesis 18).
- Abraham pleads with God to give mercy for the righteous in Sodom.
- Abraham follows God's directive to sacrifice his son Isaac (Genesis 22).
- God provides the ram in place of Isaac.

This is the type of faith Jesus found in scripture to lead him while he walked this earth. Paul gives the two foundations stones of this type of faith in Romans 4:17 - 18

> $^{17}$(as it is written, "I have made you a father of many nations"). I do this in the presence of Him whom he believed. That being **God, who gives life to the dead and calls those things that do not exist as though they did**. $^{18}$Who, contrary to hope, **in hope believed**, so

*that he became the father of many nations, according to what was spoken, "So shall your descendants be."*

First, Abraham trusted God's promise despite all contrary evidence in the physical world. When the word says, God is able, with faith to bring into our Cosmos, what does not exist now, Abraham believed. This is the foundation that Jesus spoke of when he told his disciples to demand the Cosmos yield to the greater truth within the Spiritual Realm. He stated, "Thy Kingdom come". The source of life and maintenance of life comes from Spiritual Realms. We are demanding what is true in Heavenly Realms manifest in our souls and spirits, "as it is in heaven". We are calling the victories in the Blood of Jesus to overcome all corruption in our soul bodies and physical bodies. The second foundational stone is trusting in resurrection power. To bring life from that which was dead. In Abraham's case what was dead was the womb of his wife. As recorded in Romans 4:19 – 20

> *[19]And **not being weak in faith**, he did not consider his own body, already dead (since he was about a hundred years old), and the deadness of Sarah's womb. [20]He did not waver at the promise of God through unbelief, but was **strengthened in faith, giving glory to God…***

This is the level of faith, aided by our mediator Jesus Christ we can live in while living in our physical bodies. Notice Abraham combined faith with praising God. In all things, Abraham used faith and trust to obey God. As he grew in trust and faith, he kept giving Glory to God. Humility grew in his soul as he maintained a righteous relationship with God. The more he praised and honored God the more God blessed him. Fellowship increased to the point he could trust God when God required him to sacrifice his son. All these elements happen from seeking intimacy with God. Like Abraham, we do not achieve all of this on our first attempt. God is merciful and has given us a pattern. As mentioned earlier, through applying the Redemption Blood we overcome our weaknesses.

Jesus warned us we would have troubles in this world (John 16:33). God does not create the trouble (James1:13). We are not of this world (John 15:19). We have an assignment to occupy and possess a world demons want to own. There is conflict between those who honor Jesus as King and Lord and those who do not. We learn how to lean into God's promises and words as we continue in faith. On the other side of the cross, under the Blood Covenant of Jesus, we also are learning to grow into our roles as children of God. As noted in Hebrews 12: 7 (NIV)

> *⁷Endure hardship as discipline; God is treating you as his children. For what children are not disciplined by their father?* ***⁸If you are not disciplined—and everyone undergoes discipline—then you are not legitimate, not true sons and daughters at all.*** *⁹Moreover, we have all had human fathers who disciplined us, and we respected them for it.* ***How much more should we submit to the Father of spirits and live!*** *¹⁰They disciplined us for a little while as they thought best; but God disciplines us for our good in order that we may share in his holiness.*

God's goal in reconciliation is to return us to holiness. We were created to walk with God in faith, trust and obedience. Stretching faith by living in trust and surrender may seem to take longer than we want. It is not our will, but God's will that is being accomplished. For in all things, God works for the good of those who love him (Romans 8:28). Daniel waited in prayer and in fasting twenty-one days for his answered prayer (Daniel 9). Hope is what is not seen but believed that God will provide. God is not a machine we put in prayer and draw out a reward. He is Holy! His ways and wisdom are greater than we can fathom (Isaiah 55:9). We are to stand in faith, trusting God will bring all his promises to pass. He declares there is a time and season for everything (Ecclesiastes 3:1 – 8).

God chose to create humanity to be his family. As Father he teaches his children. When we apply the Blood of Reconciliation our goal is to return to dependency on the Spiritual Realm for our life and purpose. Like Jesus, we are to be servant on God's terms, not our own understanding. So, our old ways are not only removed, but also all memories of them are obliterated! Deeper faith comes from patient endurance (James 1:2 – 4).

God's goal is to make us holy and presentable to him. Through the Blood of Reconciliation, all that was traded with Satan is in the hands of King Jesus.

These victories of Jesus are used to transform us into the likeness and image of Jesus. Jesus lives in us. The Holy Spirit also is in us through the baptism of the Holy Spirit (Romans 8:9). We have a reborn spirit that can communicate spirit to spirit with Father God in Heavenly Realms (Romans 8:14). When we align with the truth in Heavenly Realms we return to right standing and harmony with our God. As noted earlier, it is with our mouth we confess our agreement with spiritual truth (Romans 10:10). We are to stand in the same faith as Abraham, keeping our soul-hearts and spiritual eyes focused on the Spiritual Realm truths. We are to write these truths in our soul bodies. Like Abraham, we are to call out what is not seen in our Cosmos into being. To Abraham it was life in his wife's womb to bear a child. To Jesus, it was the many miracles, starting with changing water into wine. For the disciples of Jesus, it was trust and faith as they reached into the baskets to feed the thousands that more food would be there.

As Jesus told us when he gave us the keys to heaven in Matthew 16:19

*And I will give you the keys of the kingdom of heaven, and whatever you bind on earth will be bound in heaven, and whatever you loose on earth will be loosed in heaven.*

Keys are authority recognized in Heavenly Courts. Jesus is speaking about legal eternal decisions. Legal binding is agreeing with the court's ruling. All authority and dominion are in the hands of Jesus. It is when we rise in the Spiritual Realm and declare these truths we can bind them to our souls. The battles have already been won and the outcome recorded and ruling in eternity. Jesus told us by using his name, under his covenant of his Blood we have access to Spiritual Realms. He stated, in John 10:9

*I am the door. If anyone enters by Me, he will be saved and will go in and out and find pasture.*

The pasture we enter is Spiritual Realms. Notice Jesus said we would go in and out. We may enter with confidence (Hebrews 10:19 -20) to align with these victories and bind them to our soul bodies. This is operating in the faith of Abraham to call what is not visible in our Cosmos into being. What has been broken, chained, and damaged in our soul bodies, through our former lifestyle, now can be returned as if it never happened. This binding can be on a personal level or to a spiritual region.

With all things in the Spiritual Realm there is a protocol to follow. David best identified this pattern in many of his psalms. Psalm 100 is one of these that describes the method and attitude necessary to rise in the spirit and connect with the Spiritual Realm. Through the indwelling of Jesus Christ and the Holy Spirit, we may rise in our reborn spirit bodies. Psalm 100:1 – 2

> *¹Make a joyful shout to the LORD, all you lands! ²Serve the LORD with gladness; come before His presence with singing.*

We seek our God in joy and thanksgiving. So many people will shout for their favorite team when they enter a stadium. God is expecting the same level of joy as we look forward to entering his Spiritual Realm. With joy and expectation, we focus on our King Jesus. We surrender ourselves to him to serve and obey his desires. We ask Jesus to be the vine and us the branch for him to flow into us. Our intent is to honor and serve the King of Glory, Jesus Christ. Using our mouths we declare these truths in our songs.

> *³Know that the LORD, He is God; it is He who has made us, and not we ourselves; We are His people and the sheep of His pasture.*

Having spent daily time in our prayer closets and Bible study, we know who Jesus is. We start naming God's attributes and giving thanks for what he has done for us. After giving honor and joy to God with our singing, dancing and shouts, we are to recognize who we are in his presence. We declare our dependency on our God. We declare his authority as creator and our relationship as the created. We position ourselves under his care. He is our good Shepherd. We declare by his blood and his righteousness we may follow him into his courts with praise. Psalm 100:4

> *Enter His gates with thanksgiving, and into His courts with praise. Be thankful to Him and bless His name.*

Now we have access to the throne room of God. We enter in joy. We have submitted to God's will. Now we can call on our God to bring the perfect into our spirit body and soul body to overcome any darkness, corruption, and results of rebellion trying to manifest in our physical body. We call the victories of the Blood of Reconciliation to erase all that is against God. As noted in 1 John 5: 15 – 16

> *[14]Now this is the confidence that we have in Him, that if we ask anything **according to His will**, He hears us. [15]And if we know that He hears us, whatever we ask, we know that we have the petitions that we have asked of Him.*

In this process, sometimes the Holy Spirit will give us a specific Bible verse to declare. Other times, we may sense an anointing God is offering us, like bathing us in the light of God. Declare and claim whatever is being presented. Simply, "I bind to my soul" what I have just received. Finally, finish with thanksgiving and praise for what you have received. Bless God for his abundance love and provision.

When we are asking God to cleanse and purify our souls and physical bodies with the Blood of Reconciliation, we may need to complete the task multiple times. We are layering eternal truth in our souls. As noted above, the enemy still tries to attack. We fight for the truth, continually aligning with it as it is in Heavenly Realms. God's truth, his light overcomes all darkness. Jesus Christ's victories are guaranteed to be bound to our souls when we stand in faith and do not waver. As it is written, no weapon can stand against us (Isaiah 54:17)!

## Greater Peace of God

Paul explains God's form of reconciliation to the Gentiles. After telling them, they had been outside of the covenant with God, before knowing Jesus Christ as Lord and Savior, he now describes the authority in this new unity. He is not only explaining the unity between reborn Gentiles and Jewish people, but also the source and foundation of spiritual reconciliation. Ephesians 2:13 – 16

> *[13]But now in Christ Jesus you who once were far off have been brought near **by the blood of Christ**. [14]For **He Himself is our peace**. He who has made both one and has broken down the middle wall of separation. [15]**Having abolished in His flesh the enmity**. That is, the law of commandments contained in ordinances, to*

*create in Himself one new man from the two. Thus, making peace,* **¹⁶***and that He might* **reconcile them both to God in one body through the cross, thereby putting to death the enmity.**

We are a new creation in Christ (2 Corinthians 5:17). As we daily seek intimacy with Jesus Christ, the old life is exposed. As noted with the Blood of Redemption, Holy Spirit convicts us of any hidden darkness within our souls so we may bring them into the light. A deeper love bond is formed during these daily interactions with our God. A desire for greater unity is borne in our souls. This unity requires greater trust, faith and surrender of self. Our eyes are focused on the Spiritual Realm from where our sustenance comes. We seek first the perfect in the Spiritual Realms to call it into the physical realm, our Cosmos. In these acts, God moves. His peace is the gift created through applying the Blood of Reconciliation into our souls.

Before going to the cross, Jesus announced he would give his disciples his peace. As noted in John 14:27

> *"Peace, I leave with you, my peace I give to you;* ***not as the world gives do I give to you****. Let not your heart be troubled, nor let it be afraid.*

This peace or the Hebrew word "eriene", is noted in Strong's Concordance as number G1515. Its many layered meaning includes the tranquil state of the soul filled with confidence of security, prosperity, safety and fidelity. Another layer is the blessed assurance of salvation, leading to contentment in their situations in life. The peace that comes from Spiritual Realms is not simply the absence of strife. It is a living presence in the soul. After his resurrection, Jesus breathed this peace unto his disciples, as recorded in John 20:21

> *²¹So, Jesus said to them again, "Peace to you! As the Father has sent Me, I also send you." ²²And when He said this, He breathed on them, and said to them, "Receive the Holy Spirit. ²³"If you forgive the sins of any, they are forgiven them; if you retain the sins of any, they are retained."*

There are many hidden spiritual truths in the actions of Jesus recorded in this scripture. Jesus is bringing unity to those who are to be his people. He is the firstborn of the new creation. The authority and power in his resurrection blood is greater than any blood that had been previously created. To reconcile all to the original plan and purpose of God, Jesus breathes on them. As God breathed life into Adam, so now the last Adam, who is also the eternal new creation breathes new spiritual life into his disciples. What was torn asunder is reformed in this breathe by those who receive it in faith. An avenue is opened to receive in their souls a measure of the Holy Spirit. Seeds of peace, filled with confidence, assurance of salvation, and fidelity are breathed into their souls. Authority and dominion are granted them from King Jesus. The spiritual truth, of what Jesus stated in Matthew 18:18 is now active in their souls. The unity of Heavenly Realms and our Cosmos is under the dominion and authority of Jesus. In these declarations, Jesus released and renewed the authority of binding and loosing into those who operated under the authority of his Blood Covenant. With faith like Abraham, the disciples have the authority to call the perfect in Heavenly Realms to overcome and manifest into the Cosmos. They are to begin centered in their spirit bodies speaking spirit to spirit. The building of greater trust and faith allows believers to know and live this peace. These disciples were the first to receive what Jesus intends for all believers who seek him with all their hearts. As recorded in Ephesians 5:26 - 27

> *[26]That He might sanctify and cleanse her with the washing of water by the word. [27]That He might present her to Himself a glorious church, not having spot or wrinkle or any such thing, but that she should be holy and without blemish.*

The pattern described above under greater harmony is the same pattern for those seeking a greater unity with Jesus today. We look not to the physical world or human understanding for this peace. We rise daily in our spirits, seeking God. We use scripture to find answers to how to live our lives. We walk in faith, hope, and love. Thanks to God he who lives in us leads us in this way to be! As noted in Romans 8:9 – 11

> *[9]But you are not in the flesh but in the Spirit, **if indeed the Spirit of God dwells in you.** Now, if anyone does not have the Spirit of Christ, he is not His. [10]And if Christ is in you, the body is dead*

*because of sin, but the Spirit is life because of righteousness.* <sup>11</sup>*But if the Spirit of Him dwells in you, that being* **He who raised Christ from the dead will also give life to your mortal bodies through His Spirit who dwells in you.**

This deeper faith, demonstrated through functioning in one's spiritual body gives life to the physical body. When we call truth from the Spiritual Realm and then pull it into our souls then life flows into our physical body. By calling on Jesus, as the vine, and into our spirits as the branch, we can pull the authority and power of Blood of Reconciliation to align all three bodies to truth. We claim the victory of Jesus Christ over all darkness and its manifestation in our physical bodies that was embedded in our soul minds and hearts. God's truth is light that overcomes all darkness!

## The Blood of Resurrection

The newly created blood in Jesus Christ carries the attribute of resurrection. Jesus told Martha, when he was going to her brother's tomb, he is the resurrection. John recorded it in John 11:25 - 26

<sup>25</sup>*Jesus said to her,* **"I am the resurrection and the life.** *He who believes in Me, though he may die, he shall live.* <sup>26</sup>*And* **whoever lives and believes in Me** *shall never die. Do you believe this?"*

Jesus is asking us the same question, "Do we believe this?" In faith are we empowering this spiritual truth or our we empowering death? Any time we think deeply about our own death or ruin of the life as we know it, without trusting God's ways, we open the door to doubt. Satan runs in and fills it with what we deem the worst scenarios. It may be dying alone, or in a painful prolonged death. It may be not wanting to leave family members, so we let go of trusting God's ways. It may be anticipating a ruin such a possible job loss, or lifestyle change due to disasters predicted on the news media. These worries and doubts create a double-minded condition. It weighs down our souls as James described in James 1: 6 – 9

<sup>6</sup>*But let him ask in faith, with no doubting, for he who doubts is like a wave of the sea driven and tossed by the wind.* <sup>7</sup>*For let not that*

*man suppose that he will receive anything from the Lord; ⁸he is a double-minded man, unstable in all his ways.*

Before Jesus faced Gethsemane, he announced to Martha he is resurrection and life. His certainty of who he is undergirded his faith and trust in Father God to take him through the whole process and finally pouring his spiritual blood on the mercy seat in Heavenly Realms. The last barrier to walking in the faith like Jesus is the total annihilation of death from our souls. Jesus's blood accomplishes this! Our faith, trust, surrender and obedience to the truth of all his victories allows the new blood, the Blood of Resurrection to flow into us and seal us.

Look at the last part of Revelation 12:11

*And they overcame him by the blood of the Lamb and by the word of their testimony, and* **they did not love their lives to the death.**

Strong's Concordance numbers, "love their" is G25. Basically, it means "to have a preference for and regard the welfare of". "Life" in this text is translated from the Greek word, "psyche" or Strong's number G5590. Both references translate this as soul. The final access to all the authority and power in the Blood of Jesus is in not choosing my self-identity and preserving it over following the Holy Spirit. Adam's rebellion began within his soul by choosing an alternative path to knowledge. Humanity was placed in bondage in their souls because of his actions. Jesus frees us from all of this through his multiple victories over the enemy, Satan. All is recorded in the Courts of Heaven. Our risen King Jesus is the avenue for any person to gain access through faith.

Yet, it all comes back to the soul. Through the gift of free will, we may accept and enter these promises. Are we willing to surrender every protection we have built within our soul and trust God, His words, his promises and the Covenant of the Blood of Jesus? Do we truly trust that God's plans for us will overcome all we are living through at the moment? Or do we give into temptation and take back the driver's wheel and adjust the course to meet our own soul desires? When we hear from the Holy Spirit to do a specific thing, do we negotiate when and how or even delay it? Are we still seeing with our soul eyes rather than our spirit eyes? Faith, trust, surrender of self, and obedience are keys to moving within the directions of the Holy Spirit. Jesus asks, do you believe I am the resurrection and *the life?*

In Paul's letter to Timothy, he summarizes this understanding. As recorded in 2 Timothy 2:10 – 13

> *¹¹This is a faithful saying: For if we died with Him, we shall also live with Him.*
>
> *¹²If we endure, we shall also reign with Him. If we deny Him, He also will deny us.*
>
> *¹³If we are faithless, He remains faithful; He cannot deny Himself.*

Verse eleven is describing a process. The death of our former understanding, reactions, thinking, and attitudes is a gradual and continual removing of the old. As noted with the application of the other attributes of the Blood of Jesus, we work on it daily. We live in Jesus as he lives deeper in us. As the soul yields and dies to previously held beliefs, the presence of Jesus increases in our souls. As recorded in Philippians 2:12 - 13

> *¹²Therefore, my beloved, as you have always obeyed, not as in my presence only, but now much more in my absence, work out your own salvation with fear and trembling.* **¹³For it is God who works in you** *both to will and to do for His good pleasure.*

Through these daily acts of surrender, faith, trust, and obedience we apply scripture, praise, and prayer to align with the will of God for our daily lives (Philippians 4: 4 – 7). We become more than conquerors. When we fall back and deny Jesus as our Lord and seek our own ways and understanding, we cut off our souls from the fountain of life, Jesus. Thus, Paul's warning, if we deny Jesus as Lord, we will also be let go to our own ways. We may take a detour in our life as we choose to stop growing in faith and trust. We go back to self-reliance. Our hope is found in the last statement, verse thirteen. Even when we lose faith, Jesus is faithful. It is because he lives in us, he cannot deny himself. We can return to him, for Jesus and his counselor the Holy Spirit will seek to return us to his presence. This is the love our God has for his children. Even when we pull away and focus on our soul's ways, Jesus seeks us. This assurance is what is meant is the Philippians verse thirteen.

John described this process in the words of King Jesus as recorded in Revelation 3:19 – 20

> *[19] "As many as I love, I rebuke and chaste, therefore, be zealous and repent. [20] "Behold, I stand at the door and knock. If anyone hears My voice and opens the door, I will come in to him and dine with him, and he with Me."*

The love of God is so much greater than any other love we know. A parent may warn a small child of dangers and intercede when they are heading into greater danger. God does the same with his loving rebuke. He does not want more harm to come to a soul lead by willful rebellion, hurt, pain, self-indulgence or apathy. So, we are given truth and the opportunity to return to his deeper care and presence.

When we follow in greater obedience, faith and trust, God moves in our lives. The practices of seeking God above our own understanding and wisdom builds a trust like Abraham. We can call the Blood of Resurrection to pour over us daily, to break self-will, and self-dependency. When we are aware we are sacrificing ourselves for the Glory of God, the call of double mindedness through doubt fades away. Self-preservation is replaced with the greater trust in the truth of who Jesus Christ is. We ask that our will be consumed by the will of Father God. We have come full circle in the Lord's Prayer, of thy will be done in all of me as it is in Heavenly Realms. As noted in Romans 12:1

> *I beseech you therefore, brethren, by the mercies of God, that you present your bodies a living sacrifice, holy, acceptable to God, which is your reasonable service.*

All three bodies, spirit, soul, and physical bodies in alignment with the will and purpose of God as a thanksgiving sacrifice is the goal of the Blood of Resurrection. We don't accomplish this alone.

God guides us and directs us. We rest on Jesus's promise as recorded in Revelation 2:25 -26

*$^{25}$"But hold fast what you have till I come. $^{26}$"And he who overcomes, and keeps My works until the end, to him I will give power over the nations…*

We are to rise in our spirit bodies united with our source, King Jesus Christ. He is our head. One of the greatest mysteries of faith is one of the rewards for those who believe. As noted in Ephesians 2:6

*And raised us up together, and made us sit together in Christ Jesus…*

In our spirit we may rise and sit with Christ Jesus while we live in our Cosmos. John the Revelator did this as noted in the book of Revelation. When we truly embrace that King Jesus lives in us and we live in him, we walk in spirit (Galatians 5:16 -17). Greater faith and trust are created in greater obedience and death of soulish desires that focus on earthly solutions. The Blood of Resurrection facilitates this process.

# References

Thomas Nelson. NKJV, Holy Bible. Thomas Nelson. Kindle Edition.

Thomas Nelson, NIV, Holy Bible. Thomas Nelson. Kindle Edition.

Vine, W.E.Vines, Unger, Merrill & White Jr, William. Complete Expository Dictionary. (Thomas Nelson Publishers) 1996.

Blue Letter Bible Org. Published by BLB. Online application

# Other Books by Diane M. Neumann

## Available through Advantage Books

*God's Resting Place* 2025

https://www.advbookstore.com/product-page/god-s-resting-place

*Freedom Within the Kingdom of God* 2025

https://www.advbookstore.com/product-page/freedom-within-the-kingdom-of-god

*Prophetic Battle Plans* 2025

## Available through Amazon

*Weapons of Praise* 2020

*The Power of Discipleship* 2020

*Seeking God's Righteousness* 2021

*Breaking Chains Through the Power of Christ Jesus* 2021

*Grace: An Attribute of God* 2021

## Author Website

dianeneumann.com

Made in the USA
Coppell, TX
19 January 2026

68525361R00056